Cooking School

THAI

Cooking School THAI

Bring the flavours of Thailand to life in your own kitchen!

This edition published in 2011
LOVE FOOD is an imprint of Parragon Books Ltd

Parragon
Queen Street House
4 Queen Street
Bath BA1 1HE, UK

www.parragon.com

ISBN: 978-1-4454-7029-0

Printed in China

Internal design by Pink Creative

Notes for the Reader

This book uses both metric and imperial measurements. Follow the same units of measurement throughout; do not mix metric and imperial. All spoon measurements are level: teaspoons are assumed to be 5 ml, and tablespoons are assumed to be 15 ml. Unless otherwise stated, milk is assumed to be full fat, eggs and individual vegetables are medium and pepper is freshly ground black pepper.

The times given are an approximate guide only. Preparation times differ according to the techniques used by different people and the cooking times may also vary from those given. Optional ingredients, variations or serving suggestions have not been included in the calculations.

Recipes using raw or very lightly cooked eggs should be avoided by infants, the elderly, pregnant women, convalescents and anyone suffering from an illness. Pregnant and breastfeeding women are advised to avoid eating peanuts and peanut products. Sufferers from nut allergies should be aware that some of the ready-made ingredients used in the recipes in this book may contain nuts. Always check the packaging before use.

Contents

Introduction **6**

Soups and Starters **12**

Vegetables and Salads **48**

Meat **86**

Poultry **120**

Fish and Seafood **156**

Index **190**

Introduction

The pleasure of cooking and eating is at the heart of Thai life. That said, the Thais do not eat large amounts of food at any one meal. Instead they nibble away at a variety of dishes throughout the day and night. Food is easy to come by – neighbourhood restaurants, market stalls and street vendors sell a fantastic selection at affordable prices.

Rice is key to the cuisine, so much so that the Thai equivalent of 'How are you?' is 'Have you had rice today?' It is the perfect foil for the typical Thai flavours – salty, hot, sour and sweet – that give the cuisine its special character.

Regional Variations

With radical variations in topography and climate, ranging from cool mountainous peaks in the north to lush tropical forests in the south, the regions have distinctive cooking styles.

North Thailand

Bordering the southern Himalayas, this cool, remote area has limited grazing for cattle and relatively few waterways. Pork is therefore the preferred meat, while fish takes a back seat. Flavours are sharp, salty and sour, rather than searingly hot. Grilled and deep-fried foods are popular, as is sticky rice, which is sold steamed and wrapped in banana leaves.

Northeast Thailand

Hampered by poor soil and severe deforestation, the food of this region reflects the difficult conditions. Trade mark flavours are simple but robust – huge amounts of chilli, garlic, ginger, lime and fish sauce are used, tempered by generous portions of sticky rice. Because of the lack of fuel, raw or pickled foods, such as salt-preserved fish, are also a feature of the cuisine.

Central Thailand

This fertile, well-irrigated region lies at the economic and cultural heart of the country. The cooking is rich and complex, making lavish use of coconut milk, meat, freshwater fish and shellfish. Sweetness predominates, but always balanced by a salty sour element and fiery chillies.

The food from this area is the best known outside Thailand, thanks to large numbers who emigrated from the region and set up restaurants around the world. It is what we think of as typically Thai, and includes dishes such as Pad Thai, and the familiar red and green curries.

South Thailand

The food of this slender peninsula is the spiciest and most strongly flavoured in Thailand. Lethally hot bird's eye chillies, sour tamarind, unripe fruit and astringent herbs and spices are tamed by the richness of coconut – both the cream and the oil that is widely used for frying. With many miles of coastline, fish and seafood are a feature of the cuisine. Mutton, beef and chicken are popular meats, reflecting the influence of the Thai Muslims who, for religious reasons, do not eat pork.

Tips on Menu Planning

A basic Thai meal consists of rice accompanied by a soup, curry, a zesty salad and a vegetable dish. Dessert is a concept that does not exist in Thailand, though fresh fruit might finish off the meal.

You can cook as few or as many dishes as you like. It's always best to master two or three simple ones before moving on to a more ambitious menu. As a rule of thumb for a sharing menu, allow one dish per person plus rice.

Tips and Techniques

Before starting to cook

- Assemble all the ingredients, then measure or weigh them as necessary.
- Complete any preparation, such as grating and chopping.
- Cut fresh ingredients into small, equal-sized pieces so that they cook in the same amount of time. Shredding vegetables thinly and slicing them diagonally increases the surface area that comes in contact with the hot oil and speeds up cooking.
- Line up the prepared ingredients in bowls, ready to add to the cooking pot at the correct time.

Preparing spices

- Always use whole spices and grind them as needed. Once ground or crushed, spices quickly lose their distinctive aroma and flavour.
- Before grinding, dry-fry whole spices without any oil to coax out maximum flavour.
- Thai cooks use white peppercorns rather than black. These are not dry-fried as doing so imparts a bitter flavour.

Stir-frying

Do make sure the wok is very hot before you add the oil – hold your hand flat about 7 cm/2¾ inches above the base of the wok until you feel the heat. Use a long-handled ladle or tongs to constantly stir the ingredients so that they all come in contact with the hot oil and are evenly cooked.

Deep-frying

Thai cooks use less oil for deep-frying than Western cooks. Use enough to create a depth of about 2.5 cm/1 inch. Heat it over a medium–high heat until a faint haze appears. If the oil is not hot enough, the food will soak it up and become soggy. Cook in small batches to avoid overcrowding the pan. Remove the food with tongs and drain on kitchen paper.

Cooking Equipment

You don't need specialist equipment to produce authentic Thai food. However, the following items are important.

MORTAR AND PESTLE

The most indispensable item is a large mortar and pestle, preferably made from rough stone such as granite. Thai cooks use them for grinding, crushing or mashing spices, fresh herbs, fibrous roots and other ingredients to make relishes and curry pastes.

SPICE GRINDER

A small spice grinder (or electric coffee grinder kept especially for the purpose) is useful for grinding large amounts of spice.

WOK

With its conical shape, the wok is the best pan to use for stir-frying. Thanks to the outward-sloping sides, the food constantly falls back to the centre where the heat is most intense. If fitted with a lid and a stand for stability, the wok can also be used for curries and deep-fried dishes.

Ingredients

You will need basic seasonings, oils and various other store-cupboard items, many of which you will already have. Commonly used ingredients, such as limes, fresh ginger, garlic and coconut milk, are easily found in supermarkets. The more unusual items are sold in Thai shops, by mail order or on the internet. It's worth stocking up with these as they will give your cooking that authentic Thai flavour.

Unopened cans and jars will keep for months in a store cupboard and for several weeks in the refrigerator once opened. Fresh items, such as kaffir lime leaves, coriander root and galangal, can all be frozen until needed.

AUBERGINES

Thai aubergines are different from the purple Mediterranean variety. There are three types: marble-sized green 'pea' aubergines, slightly larger oval white ones and the round green 'apple' aubergine. They are all clean tasting and crisp, and are eaten raw or lightly cooked.

If necessary, diced purple aubergine can be used instead, but the texture will be softer and the colour lacking.

CHILLIES

Thai chillies are small and lethally hot. The very hottest are the 'mouse-dropping' chillies, which are about 1 cm/½ inch long. Almost as hot are the slightly larger 'bird's eye' chillies. Red chillies are riper versions of green ones and are marginally milder. Chillies will keep for several weeks in the refrigerator stored in a polythene bag.

CORIANDER ROOT

Asian shops sell big bunches of fresh coriander with the roots attached. Don't throw these away – they are a vital ingredient in sauces and curry pastes. If not needed immediately, cut off the leaves and store the roots in a sealed polythene bag in the freezer.

FISH SAUCE

Known as 'nam pla' in Thailand, fish sauce is a thin brown liquid made by fermenting fish with salt. It has a pungent, almost rotten aroma, but adds a special richness and flavour to foods. It is diluted in dipping sauces, and is used at the table in the same way as salt.

GALANGAL

Recognizable by its translucent gold skin, galangal is used like ginger but has a sharper, more peppery flavour. Found mainly in Asian shops, the fresh root can be stored in the refrigerator for several weeks or frozen until needed. Chopped galangal is sold in jars but the flavour is inferior to the fresh root.

KAFFIR LIME LEAVES

These are glossy dark green leaves that grow in pairs. They have a unique lemon-lime flavour and are used in the same way as bay leaves. Fresh or frozen leaves have a much better flavour than dried.

LEMON GRASS

This lemon-scented grass has a cool refreshing flavour that counteracts the heat of chillies in soups, curries and spice pastes. It has a long woody stalk with fibrous leaves and a white bulbous stem end. Peel away the coarse outer layers before chopping or pounding.

PALM SUGAR

Sold in discs, cones or cylinders, palm sugar has a rich caramel-like flavour. It is used not only in sweet dishes, but also in savoury dishes to counteract the saltiness of soy and fish sauce, and to temper the heat of chillies. If it is rock-hard, use a vegetable peeler to shave off bits.

SHRIMP PASTE

Made from a particular kind of fermented, salted and sun-dried shrimp, this imparts an essential Thai flavour to curry pastes, marinades and sauces. Don't be put off by the overpowering aroma – it disappears once heated. Keep the paste in the refrigerator in a very well-sealed container.

Thai Curries

Thailand is justly famous for its fresh-tasting curries, made from aromatic pastes of mashed chillies, fresh herbs and roots, fish sauce and other seasonings. The classics are green curry, red curry, the sweet-sour 'masaman' curry and the milder Penang curry. Curry pastes are sold ready made (look for the Thai brands sold in Thai shops) but it's hard to beat home-made pastes for flavour and vibrant colour. They can be kept in a screw-top jar in the refrigerator for up to a week.

GREEN CURRY PASTE
Makes 175 ml/6 fl oz

1 tbsp coriander seeds

½ tbsp cumin seeds

1 tsp white peppercorns, crushed

4 tbsp water

12 fresh bird's eye chillies, deseeded and chopped

5 garlic cloves, chopped

2 lemon grass stalks, coarse outer leaves discarded, chopped

5 fresh or frozen kaffir lime leaves, chopped

70 g/2½ oz fresh coriander leaves, chopped

finely grated zest of 1 lime

Heat a frying pan until hot, add the coriander seeds and dry-fry over a medium–high heat, shaking the pan frequently, for 2 minutes, or until starting to pop. Dry-fry the cumin seeds for 30 seconds, or until fragrant, taking care not to let them burn.

Grind the toasted seeds and the peppercorns to a coarse powder, using a mortar and pestle. Put the powder and all the remaining ingredients in a blender, and process for 2–3 minutes to a thick, smooth paste, scraping down the goblet several times. Transfer to a screw-top glass jar and store in the refrigerator for up to a week.

RED CURRY PASTE
Makes 175 ml/6 fl oz

12 dried red chillies, deseeded

1 tbsp coriander seeds

½ tbsp cumin seeds

1 tsp white peppercorns, crushed

6 tbsp water

2 shallots, chopped

2.5-cm/1-inch piece fresh ginger, chopped

2 lemon grass stalks, coarse outer leaves discarded, chopped

4 fresh or frozen Kaffir lime leaves, chopped

1 tbsp chopped coriander root, or 1 extra tsp coriander seeds

finely grated zest of 1 lime

1 tsp salt

Put the chillies in a small bowl, cover with boiling water and leave them to soak for 15 minutes until pliable. Drain and set aside.

Heat a frying pan until hot, add the coriander seeds and dry-fry over a medium–high heat, shaking the pan frequently, for 2 minutes, or until starting to pop. Dry-fry the cumin seeds for 30 seconds, or until fragrant, taking care not to let them burn.

Grind the toasted seeds and the peppercorns to a coarse powder, using a mortar and pestle. Put the powder and all the remaining ingredients in a blender, and process for 2–3 minutes to a thick, smooth paste, scraping down the goblet several times. Transfer to a screw-top glass jar and store in the refrigerator for up to a week.

Soups and Starters

Thai meals are not divided into separate courses as they are in the West. Soups and small dishes with which we would normally begin the meal are put on the table along with all the other dishes. Since there is no prescribed order of eating, soups are enjoyed throughout the meal and are used to balance flavours. For example Hot-and-sour Soup would be good before or after a meat dish with a sweet flavour, and the simple Pork and Vegetable Broth would counteract the richness of a masaman curry. Substantial noodle-based soups, such as Spicy Prawn Soup, are meals in themselves and can be served Western-style, with nothing more than a zesty salad.

Thais also enjoy a selection of small dishes with drinks, served well before the main meal in order not to spoil the appetite. 'Starters' are also eaten at any time of day – first thing in the morning, as a mid-morning snack or as a mid-afternoon pick-me-up.

Typical small dishes include delectable Crispy Sesame Prawns and Thai Crab Cakes. There are also irresistible satays, spicy wontons and spring rolls. These are, in fact, Chinese in origin, but have spread throughout South-East Asia. They are surprisingly substantial and on their own would make an excellent meze-like meal for sharing with friends, or even a Thai-style Sunday brunch.

Beef and Noodle Soup

SERVES 4

4 shallots, chopped

1 large garlic clove, chopped

2 tsp finely chopped fresh ginger

1 tbsp groundnut oil

450 g/1 lb sirloin steak,
   external fat removed,
   cut into 1-cm/½-inch cubes

1.3 litres/2¼ pints spicy beef stock

1 tsp white peppercorns, crushed

150 g/5½ oz flat rice noodles

juice of 1 lime

2 tsp Thai fish sauce

½ tsp salt

½ tsp sugar

TO GARNISH

4 spring onions, shredded

slivers of red chilli

3 tbsp torn coriander leaves

3 tbsp torn basil leaves

lime wedges

1. Place the shallots, garlic and ginger in a food processor or blender and pulse several times until a fairly smooth paste forms.

2. Heat a wok over a medium–high heat, then add the oil and stir-fry the paste for 2 minutes, taking care not to let it burn. Add the beef and stir-fry for 1 minute until browned, then pour in 1 litre/1¾ pints of the stock. Bring to a rolling boil, skimming off any scum that forms. Add the crushed peppercorns, then reduce the heat and gently simmer for 30–35 minutes, or until the meat is tender.

3. Meanwhile, soak the noodles for 15 minutes in enough lukewarm water to cover, or cook according to the instructions on the packet, until soft.

4. When the meat is tender, stir in any sticky residue that has formed at the edge of the wok. Add the remaining stock, the lime juice, fish sauce, salt and sugar. Simmer for a few minutes.

5. Drain the noodles and divide between four warmed soup bowls. Ladle the meat and broth over the top. Serve with the garnishes sprinkled over the soup.

Pork and Vegetable Broth

SERVES 4

1 tbsp chilli oil

1 garlic clove, chopped

3 spring onions, sliced

1 red pepper, deseeded and finely
   sliced

2 tbsp cornflour

1 litre/1¾ pints vegetable stock

1 tbsp soy sauce

2 tbsp rice wine or dry sherry

150 g/5½ oz pork fillet, sliced

1 tbsp finely chopped lemon grass

1 small red chilli, deseeded and finely
   chopped

1 tbsp grated fresh ginger

115 g/4 oz fine egg noodles

200 g/7 oz canned water chestnuts,
   drained and sliced

salt and pepper

1. Heat the oil in a large saucepan. Add the garlic and spring onions and cook over
   a medium heat, stirring, for 3 minutes until slightly soft. Add the red pepper and
   cook for a further 5 minutes, stirring.

2. In a bowl, mix the cornflour with enough of the stock to make a smooth paste,
   then stir it into the pan. Cook, stirring, for 2 minutes. Stir in the remaining stock,
   the soy sauce and the rice wine, then add the pork, lemon grass, chilli and ginger.
   Season with salt and pepper. Bring to the boil, then reduce the heat and simmer
   for 25 minutes.

3. Bring a separate saucepan of water to the boil, add the noodles and cook for
   3 minutes. Remove from the heat, drain, then add the noodles to the soup along
   with the water chestnuts. Cook for a further 2 minutes, then remove from the heat
   and ladle into warmed bowls.

Chicken Noodle Soup

SERVES 4

1 tbsp sesame oil or chilli oil

2 garlic cloves, chopped

2 spring onions, trimmed and sliced

1 leek, trimmed and finely sliced

1 tbsp grated fresh ginger

1 fresh red chilli, deseeded and finely chopped

350 g/12 oz skinless, boneless chicken breasts, cut into strips

900 ml/1½ pints chicken stock

2 tbsp rice wine

1 tbsp chopped lemon grass

6 kaffir lime leaves, finely shredded

200 g/7 oz fine egg noodles

salt and pepper

1. Heat the oil in a wok or large saucepan. Add the garlic and cook over a medium heat, stirring, for 1 minute, then add the spring onions, leek, ginger and chilli and cook, stirring, for a further 3 minutes. Add the chicken, stock and rice wine, bring to the boil and simmer for 20 minutes. Stir in the lemon grass and kaffir lime leaves.

2. Bring a separate saucepan of water to the boil and add the noodles. Cook for 3 minutes, drain well, then add to the soup. Season to taste with salt and pepper. Cook for a further 2 minutes. Remove from the heat, ladle into individual warmed bowls and serve hot.

Chicken-coconut Soup

SERVES 4

115 g/4 oz dried vermicelli noodles

1.2 litres/2 pints chicken stock or vegetable stock

1 lemon grass stalk, crushed

1-cm/½-inch piece fresh ginger, peeled and very finely chopped

2 fresh kaffir lime leaves, thinly sliced

1 fresh red chilli, or to taste, deseeded and thinly sliced

2 skinless, boneless chicken breasts, thinly sliced

200 ml/7 fl oz coconut cream

2–3 tbsp Thai fish sauce

1–2 tbsp fresh lime juice

55 g/2 oz beansprouts

4 spring onions, green part only, finely sliced

fresh coriander leaves, to garnish

1. Soak the dried noodles in a large bowl with enough lukewarm water to cover for 20 minutes, until soft. Alternatively, cook according to the packet instructions. Drain well and set aside.

2. Meanwhile, bring the stock to the boil in a large saucepan over a high heat. Reduce the heat, add the lemon grass, ginger, lime leaves and chilli and simmer for 5 minutes. Add the chicken and continue simmering for a further 3 minutes, or until cooked. Stir in the coconut cream, fish sauce and 1 tablespoon of the lime juice, and continue to simmer for 3 minutes. Add the beansprouts and spring onions and simmer for a further minute. Taste and add more fish sauce or lime juice, if needed. Remove and discard the lemon grass stalk.

3. Divide the vermicelli noodles between four warmed bowls. Bring the soup back to the boil, then add to each bowl. The heat of the soup will warm the noodles. To garnish, sprinkle with coriander leaves.

Duck with Spring Onion Soup

SERVES 2

2 duck breasts, skin on

2 tbsp Red Curry Paste (see page 11)

2 tbsp vegetable oil or groundnut oil

bunch of spring onions, chopped

2 garlic cloves, crushed

5-cm/2-inch piece fresh ginger, grated

2 carrots, thinly sliced

1 red pepper, deseeded and cut into strips

1 litre/1¾ pints chicken stock

2 tbsp sweet chilli sauce

3–4 tbsp Thai soy sauce

400 g/14 oz canned straw mushrooms, drained

1. Slash the skin of the duck three or four times with a sharp knife and rub in the curry paste. Cook the duck breasts, skin-side down, in a wok or frying pan over a high heat for 2–3 minutes. Turn over, reduce the heat and cook for a further 3–4 minutes, until cooked through. Lift out and slice thickly. Set aside and keep warm.

2. Meanwhile, heat the oil in a wok or large frying pan and stir-fry half the spring onions, the garlic, ginger, carrots and red pepper for 2–3 minutes. Pour in the stock and add the chilli sauce, soy sauce and mushrooms. Bring to the boil, reduce the heat and simmer for 4–5 minutes.

3. Ladle the soup into warmed bowls, top with the duck slices and garnish with the remaining spring onions. Serve immediately.

Spicy Prawn Soup

SERVES 4

1 tbsp sunflower oil

2–3 garlic cloves, cut into thin slivers

1–2 fresh red Thai chillies, deseeded and sliced

2 lemon grass stalks, outer leaves removed, chopped

2.5-cm/1-inch piece fresh ginger, grated

1.2 litres/2 pints fish or vegetable stock

350 g/12 oz large raw prawns, peeled and deveined

115 g/4 oz shiitake mushrooms, sliced

1 large carrot, grated

55 g/2 oz dried egg noodles (optional)

1–2 tsp Thai fish sauce

1 tbsp chopped fresh coriander

1. Heat the oil in a large saucepan over a medium heat, add the garlic, chillies, lemon grass and ginger and cook for 5 minutes, stirring frequently. Add the stock and bring to the boil, then reduce the heat and simmer for 5 minutes.

2. Stir in the prawns, mushrooms and carrot. If using the egg noodles, break into small lengths, add to the saucepan and simmer for a further 5 minutes, or until the prawns have turned pink and the noodles are tender.

3. Stir in the fish sauce and coriander and heat through for a further minute before serving in warmed bowls.

Tom Yum Soup with Fish

SERVES 6

1.5 litres/2½ pints light chicken stock

6 lemon grass stalks, crushed to release their flavour

3 tbsp very finely chopped coriander roots

10 kaffir lime leaves, central stalks torn off

1 red chilli, deseeded and finely chopped

2.5-cm/1-inch piece galangal or fresh ginger, peeled and thinly sliced

3 tbsp Thai fish sauce, plus extra to taste

1 tbsp sugar, plus extra to taste

500 g/1 lb 2 oz raw prawns, shelled except for the tails

500 g/1 lb 2 oz firm white fish, such as cod or monkfish, chopped into bite-sized pieces

225 g/8 oz canned bamboo shoots or water chestnuts

12 cherry tomatoes, halved

juice of 2 limes

handful of fresh coriander leaves and handful of fresh Thai basil leaves, chopped, to garnish

1. Pour the stock into a large saucepan and add the lemon grass, coriander roots, lime leaves, chilli, galangal, fish sauce and sugar. Cover the saucepan. Bring to the boil, then reduce the heat and simmer for 10 minutes.

2. Add the prawns, fish and bamboo shoots and simmer for a further 4 minutes. Add the tomatoes and lime juice and check the seasoning, adding more fish sauce and sugar, if necessary.

3. Remove and discard the lemon grass stalks, then divide the soup between six warmed bowls and scatter over the coriander and basil leaves.

Hot-and-Sour Soup

SERVES 4

2 fresh red chillies, deseeded
  and roughly chopped

6 tbsp rice vinegar

1.2 litres/2 pints vegetable stock

2 lemon grass stalks, halved

4 tbsp soy sauce

1 tbsp palm sugar

juice of ½ lime

2 tbsp groundnut oil or vegetable oil

225 g/8 oz firm tofu (drained weight),
  cut into 1-cm/½-inch cubes

400 g/14 oz canned straw mushrooms,
  drained

4 spring onions, chopped

1 small head pak choi, shredded

1. Mix the chillies and vinegar together in a non-metallic bowl, cover and leave to stand at room temperature for 1 hour.

2. Meanwhile, bring the stock to the boil in a saucepan. Add the lemon grass, soy sauce, sugar and lime juice, reduce the heat and simmer for 20–30 minutes.

3. Heat the oil in a preheated wok, add the tofu and stir-fry over a high heat for 2–3 minutes, or until browned all over. (You may need to do this in two batches, depending on the size of the wok.) Remove with a slotted spoon and drain on kitchen paper.

4. Add the chillies and vinegar with the tofu, mushrooms and half the spring onions to the stock mixture and cook for 10 minutes. Mix the remaining spring onions with the pak choi and scatter over the soup before serving.

Spicy Beef and Mushroom Wontons

MAKES 12–15

12–15 square wonton wrappers
groundnut oil, for deep-frying
soy-ginger dipping sauce, to serve

FILLING
125 g/4 oz lean sirloin steak or rump
    steak, minced
1 spring onion, green part included,
    finely chopped
2 button mushrooms, finely chopped

1 small garlic clove, finely chopped
½ tsp finely chopped fresh ginger
½ tsp soy sauce
¼ tsp salt
¼ tsp pepper
⅛ tsp five-spice powder
½ tsp cornflour
1 egg, beaten
chopped spring onion, to garnish

1. To make the filling, combine the steak, spring onion, mushrooms, garlic and ginger in a bowl. Mix the soy sauce, salt, pepper, five-spice powder and cornflour to a thin paste. Add the paste to the beef mixture, then stir in half the beaten egg (use the remainder in another recipe). Stir with a fork until very well mixed.

2. Separate the wonton squares and place on a tray, rotating them so one corner is facing towards you. Cover with a clean damp tea towel to prevent cracking. Working with one square at a time, place a slightly rounded teaspoon of filling in the bottom corner 1 cm/½ inch away from the point. Fold the point over the filling, then roll up two thirds of the wrapper, leaving a point at the top. Moisten the right- and left-hand corners with a dab of water. Fold one corner over the other and press lightly to seal into a bishop's mitre shape. Continue until all the wontons are filled.

3. Heat a large wok over a high heat. Pour in the oil and heat to 180–190°C/350–375°F, or until a cube of bread browns in 30 seconds. Deep-fry the wontons in batches for 4–5 minutes until golden brown. Remove with tongs and drain on kitchen paper. Garnish with chopped spring onion and serve with the soy-ginger dipping sauce.

Crispy Pork Dumplings

SERVES 4

3 spring onions, roughly chopped

1 garlic clove, roughly chopped

1 small fresh red chilli, deseeded and
   roughly chopped

250 g/9 oz minced pork

1 tsp salt

20 wonton wrappers

groundnut oil or vegetable oil,
   for deep-frying

chillies, cut in to flowers, to garnish

1. Put the spring onions, garlic, chilli, pork and salt in a food processor and process to
   a smooth paste.

2. Remove the wonton wrappers from the packet, but keep them in a pile and cover
   with a clean, damp tea towel to prevent them drying out. Lay one wrapper on a
   work surface in front of you in a diamond shape and brush the edges with water.
   Put a small amount of filling near one edge and fold the wrapper over the filling.
   Press the edges together to seal the parcel and shape into a semicircle like a pasty.
   Repeat with the remaining wrappers and filling.

3. Heat the oil in a wok, deep saucepan or deep-fat fryer to 180–190°C/
   350–375°F, or until a cube of bread browns in 30 seconds. Add the dumplings,
   in batches, and cook for 45 seconds–1 minute until crisp and golden all over.
   Remove with a slotted spoon, drain on kitchen paper and keep warm while you
   cook the remaining dumplings. Serve immediately, garnished with chilli flowers.

Pork and Prawn Spring Rolls

MAKES 25

6 dried Chinese mushrooms, soaked in warm water for 20 minutes

1 tbsp vegetable oil or groundnut oil, plus extra for deep-frying

225 g/8 oz minced pork

1 tsp dark soy sauce

100 g/3½ oz canned bamboo shoots, rinsed and cut into julienne strips

pinch of salt

100 g/3½ oz prawns, peeled, deveined and chopped

225 g/8 oz fresh beansprouts, roughly chopped

1 tbsp finely chopped spring onions

25 spring roll wrappers

1 egg white, lightly beaten

chilli sauce, to serve

1. Squeeze out any excess water from the mushrooms and finely slice, discarding any tough stems.

2. Heat a wok over a medium–high heat, then add the oil. Add the pork and stir-fry until it changes colour. Add the soy sauce, bamboo shoots, mushrooms and salt. Stir over a high heat for 3 minutes.

3. Add the prawns and cook for 2 minutes, then add the beansprouts and cook for a further minute. Remove from the heat, stir in the spring onions and set aside to cool.

4. Place a tablespoon of the mixture towards the bottom of a spring roll wrapper. Roll once to secure the filling, then fold in the sides to create a 10-cm/4-inch width and continue to roll up. Seal with egg white.

5. Heat a large wok over a high heat. Pour in the oil and heat to 180–190°C/ 350–375°F, or until a cube of bread browns in 30 seconds. Without overcrowding the pan, fry the rolls for about 5 minutes, until golden brown and crispy. Drain well on kitchen paper and serve immediately with chilli sauce.

Chicken Satay Skewers

SERVES 4

4 skinless, boneless chicken breasts, about 115 g/4 oz each, cut into 2-cm/¾-inch cubes

4 tbsp soy sauce

1 tbsp cornflour

2 garlic cloves, finely chopped

2.5-cm/1-inch piece fresh ginger, peeled and finely chopped

cucumber, roughly chopped, to serve

PEANUT SAUCE

2 tbsp groundnut oil

½ onion, finely chopped

1 garlic clove, finely chopped

4 tbsp crunchy peanut butter

4–5 tbsp water

½ tsp chilli powder

1. Put the chicken in a shallow dish. Mix the soy sauce, cornflour, garlic and ginger together in a small bowl and pour over the chicken. Cover and leave to marinate in the refrigerator for at least 2 hours. Meanwhile, soak 12 bamboo skewers in cold water for at least 30 minutes.

2. Preheat the oven to 190°C/375°F/Gas Mark 5. Divide the chicken cubes between the bamboo skewers. Heat a ridged griddle pan until hot, add the skewers and cook over a high heat for 3–4 minutes, turning occasionally, until browned all over. Transfer the skewers to a baking sheet and cook in the preheated oven for 5–8 minutes until cooked through.

3. Meanwhile, to make the sauce, heat the oil in a saucepan, add the onion and garlic and cook over a medium heat, stirring frequently, for 3–4 minutes until soft. Add the peanut butter, water and chilli powder and simmer for 2–3 minutes until softened and thinned.

4. Serve the skewers immediately with the warm sauce and the cucumber.

Crab Cakes

SERVES 6

300 g/10½ oz canned crabmeat, drained

1–2 fresh bird's eye chillies, deseeded and finely chopped

6 spring onions, trimmed and thinly sliced

140 g/5 oz courgettes, grated

115 g/4 oz carrot, peeled and grated

1 tbsp chopped fresh coriander

2 tbsp cornflour

2 egg whites

1 spray sunflower oil

150 ml/5 fl oz low-fat natural yogurt

Tabasco sauce, to taste

2 tsp sesame seeds

lime wedges, to garnish

1. Place the crabmeat in a bowl and stir in the chillies, spring onions, grated courgette, carrot and coriander. Add the cornflour and mix well.

2. Beat the egg whites together in a separate bowl then stir into the crab mixture and mix together.

3. Heat a non-stick frying pan and lightly spray with the oil, then drop small spoonfuls of the crab mixture into the pan. Fry the crab cakes over a low heat for 3–4 minutes, pressing down with the back of a spatula. Turn over halfway through cooking. Cook the crab cakes in batches.

4. Mix the yogurt and Tabasco sauce in a small bowl and stir in the sesame seeds. Spoon into a small bowl and use as a dipping sauce with the cooked crab cakes. Serve garnished with lime wedges, divided equally between six plates.

Crispy Sesame Prawns

SERVES 4

115 g/4 oz self-raising flour

3 tbsp sesame seeds, toasted or
  dry-fried

1 tsp Red Curry Paste (see page 11)

1 tbsp Thai fish sauce

150 ml/5 fl oz water

vegetable oil or groundnut oil,
  for deep-frying

20 large, uncooked prawns,
  peeled, with tails intact

fresh coriander sprigs, to garnish

chilli sauce, to serve

1. Combine the flour and sesame seeds in a bowl. Stir together the curry paste,
    fish sauce and water in a jug until mixed. Gradually pour the liquid into the flour,
    stirring constantly, to make a thick batter.

2. Heat a large wok over a high heat. Pour in the oil and heat to 180–190°C/
    350–375°F, or until a cube of bread browns in 30 seconds. Holding the prawns
    by their tails, dip them into the batter, one at a time, then carefully drop into the
    hot oil. Cook for 2–3 minutes, until crisp and browned. Drain on kitchen paper.

3. Garnish with fresh coriander sprigs and serve immediately with chilli sauce.

Spicy Parcels

SERVES 4

OMELETTES

4 eggs

2 tbsp water

3 spring onions, finely chopped

small handful of fresh coriander, finely chopped

groundnut oil or vegetable oil, for shallow-frying

soy sauce, to serve

FILLING

3 spring onions, roughly chopped

225 g/8 oz raw squid, cleaned and cut into chunks if large or rings if small

115 g/4 oz raw prawns, peeled and deveined

115 g/4 oz skinned white fish fillet, such as cod or coley, cut into 2.5-cm/1-inch cubes

1 head pak choi, roughly chopped

1 tbsp Green Curry Paste (see page 11)

1 tsp Thai fish sauce

1. Preheat the oven to 190°C/375°F/Gas Mark 5. For the omelettes, beat the eggs, water, spring onions and half the coriander together in a bowl. Heat 1 tablespoon of oil in a 20-cm/8-inch non-stick frying pan. Drizzle a quarter of the egg mixture over the base of the frying pan to make a rough lacy pattern. Cook over a medium–high heat for 2 minutes, or until just set, then use a palette knife to turn the omelette over and cook on the other side for 1 minute. Slide out onto a plate or chopping board. Repeat with the remaining mixture to make three more omelettes and add to the plate or board. Set aside and keep warm.

2. For the filling, heat 1 tablespoon of oil in the frying pan, add the spring onions and all the seafood and cook over a medium heat, stirring frequently, for 2–3 minutes until the squid is firm, the prawns have turned pink and the fish is just cooked through. Transfer to a food processor and process for 30 seconds, or until just mixed. Add the pak choi, the remaining coriander, the curry paste and fish sauce and process again to a coarse mixture.

3. Arrange the omelettes on a chopping board and put a quarter of the seafood mixture in the centre of each. Roll one side of each omelette over the filling, fold in the adjacent 'sides' to cover the filling, then fold up the omelette to make a small, square parcel. Transfer the parcels to a baking sheet.

4. Bake in the preheated oven for 10–15 minutes until lightly browned and cooked through. Serve immediately with soy sauce.

Vegetable and Black Bean Spring Rolls

SERVES 4

2 tbsp groundnut oil or vegetable oil, plus extra for deep-frying

4 spring onions, cut into 5-cm/2-inch lengths and shredded lengthways

2.5-cm/1-inch piece fresh ginger, peeled and finely chopped

1 large carrot, peeled and cut into matchsticks

1 red pepper, deseeded and cut into matchsticks

6 tbsp black bean sauce

55 g/2 oz fresh beansprouts

200 g/7 oz canned water chestnuts, drained and roughly chopped

5-cm/2-inch piece cucumber, cut into matchsticks

8 x 20-cm/8-inch square spring roll wrappers

1. Heat the oil in a preheated wok, add the spring onions, ginger, carrot and red pepper and stir-fry over a medium–high heat for 2–3 minutes. Add the black bean sauce, beansprouts, water chestnuts and cucumber and stir-fry for 1–2 minutes. Leave to cool.

2. Remove the spring roll wrappers from the packet, but keep them in a pile and cover with a clean, damp tea towel to prevent them drying out. Lay one wrapper on a work surface in front of you in a diamond shape and brush the edges with water. Put a spoonful of the filling near one corner and fold the corner over the filling. Roll over again and then fold the side corners over the filling. Roll up to seal the filling completely. Repeat with the remaining wrappers and filling.

3. Heat the oil for deep-frying in a wok, deep saucepan or deep-fat fryer to 180–190°C/350–375°F, or until a cube of bread browns in 30 seconds. Add the rolls, in 2–3 batches, and cook for 2–3 minutes until crisp and golden all over. Remove with a slotted spoon, drain on kitchen paper and keep warm while you cook the remaining rolls. Serve immediately.

Vegetables and Salads

Thanks to the varying climate, Thailand produces an impressive variety of vegetables, many of them used in the West and some that are not so familiar. Cooked or raw vegetables accompany every meal, mitigating the heat of the chillies used in many dishes and providing welcome texture and colour.

Cabbages, cucumber and carrots are popular, either raw in salads and relishes, or lightly cooked in a stir-fry. There are various types of green bean: winged beans, which taste something like asparagus, and yard-long or snake beans, which are similar in flavour to ordinary French beans. Thai pea aubergines and round 'apple' aubergines are a key ingredient, adding colour and crunch to stir-fries and curries. Freshness is paramount, and every part of the vegetable, including shoots and roots that Western cooks might discard, is used.

Unlike the soft leafy salads of the West, Thai salads are an exciting mix of substantial ingredients with bold flavours and distinct textures. Beef and poultry often form the basis, as do oily fish, such as tuna – try the mouthwatering Caramelized Tuna Salad or the zesty Gingered Chicken and Vegetable Salad. Sharp-tasting fruits, such as pomelo (a type of grapefruit) and green mango, are also a feature of many of the salads, giving even more freshness to a refreshing plate.

Dressings range from the clean sharp flavours of lime juice, fish sauce and chilli, to more complex concoctions, which may include ginger and sesame oil. Fresh herbs, such as mint, basil and coriander, are used in abundance rather than for sprinkling or as a garnish when serving.

Mixed Vegetables with Basil

SERVES 4

2 tbsp vegetable oil or groundnut oil,
  plus extra for shallow frying

2 garlic cloves, chopped

1 onion, sliced

115 g/4 oz baby corn, cut in half
  diagonally

½ cucumber, peeled, halved,
  deseeded and sliced

225 g/8 oz canned water chestnuts,
  drained and rinsed

55 g/2 oz mangetout

115 g/4 oz shiitake mushrooms, halved

1 red pepper, deseeded and
  thinly sliced

1 tbsp soft light brown sugar

2 tbsp Thai soy sauce

1 tbsp Thai fish sauce

1 tbsp rice vinegar

8–12 sprigs fresh Thai basil

freshly cooked plain rice, to serve

1. Heat a wok over a high heat, then add the oil. Add the garlic and onion and stir-fry for 1–2 minutes. Add the baby corn, cucumber, water chestnuts, mangetout, mushrooms and red pepper and stir-fry for 2–3 minutes, until starting to soften.

2. Add the sugar, soy sauce, fish sauce and vinegar and gradually bring to the boil. Simmer for 1–2 minutes.

3. Meanwhile, heat enough oil for shallow frying in a wok and, when hot, add the basil sprigs. Cook for 20–30 seconds until crisp. Remove with a slotted spoon and drain on kitchen paper.

4. Garnish the vegetable stir-fry with the crispy basil and serve immediately with rice.

Broccoli with Peanuts

SERVES 4

3 tbsp vegetable oil or groundnut oil

1 lemon grass stem, roughly chopped

2 fresh red chillies, deseeded and chopped

2.5-cm/1-inch piece fresh ginger, grated

3 kaffir lime leaves, roughly torn

3 tbsp Green Curry Paste (see page 11)

1 onion, chopped

1 red pepper, deseeded and chopped

350 g/12 oz broccoli, cut into florets

115 g/4 oz French beans

55 g/2 oz unsalted peanuts

1. Put 2 tablespoons of the oil, the lemon grass, chillies, ginger, lime leaves and curry paste into a food processor or blender and process to a paste.

2. Heat a wok over a medium heat and add the remaining oil. Add the spice paste, onion and red pepper and stir-fry for 2–3 minutes, until the vegetables start to soften.

3. Add the broccoli and beans, cover and cook over a low heat, stirring occasionally, for 4–5 minutes, until tender.

4. Meanwhile, toast or dry-fry the peanuts until lightly browned. Add them to the broccoli mixture and toss together. Serve immediately.

Cauliflower and Beans with Cashew Nuts

SERVES 4

1 tbsp vegetable oil or groundnut oil

1 tbsp chilli oil

1 onion, chopped

2 garlic cloves, chopped

2 tbsp Red Curry Paste (see page 11)

1 small cauliflower, cut into florets

175 g/6 oz runner beans,
   cut into 7.5-cm/3-inch lengths

150 ml/5 fl oz vegetable stock

2 tbsp Thai soy sauce

50 g/1¾ oz toasted cashew nuts,
   to garnish

1. Heat the vegetable oil and chilli oil in a wok, add the onion and garlic and stir-fry until soft. Add the curry paste and stir-fry for 1–2 minutes.

2. Add the cauliflower and beans and stir-fry for 3–4 minutes, until soft. Pour in the stock and soy sauce and simmer for 1–2 minutes. Serve immediately, garnished with the cashew nuts.

Mushroom and Tofu Laksa with Noodles

SERVES 4

850 ml/1½ pints vegetable stock

400 ml/14 fl oz coconut milk

250 g/9 oz shiitake mushrooms, stalks removed, thinly sliced

150 g/5¼ oz firm tofu, cubed

2 tbsp tomato purée

175 g/6 oz fine egg noodles

salt and pepper

8 spring onions, sliced, and 4 tbsp shredded mint leaves, to garnish

lime wedges, to serve

SPICE PASTE

2 red chillies, deseeded and chopped

4-cm/1½-inch piece fresh ginger, chopped

2 large garlic cloves, chopped

2 lemon grass stems, tough outer layers removed, inner stalks chopped

1 tsp coriander seeds, crushed

6 macadamia nuts, chopped

small handful of coriander leaves

3 tbsp vegetable oil

1. Purée the spice paste ingredients in a food processor, pulsing several times until smooth.

2. Heat a wok over a medium–high heat, add the spice paste and stir-fry for 30 seconds. Pour in the stock and coconut milk, and bring to the boil. Add the mushrooms, tofu and tomato purée and season with salt and pepper. Simmer gently for 5 minutes.

3. Bring a large saucepan of lightly salted water to the boil, add the noodles and cook for 4 minutes, or according to the instructions on the packet, until soft. Divide between four large warmed soup bowls. Ladle the spicy broth over the noodles. Garnish with sliced spring onions and shredded mint leaves and serve with lime wedges.

Vegetable Stir-fry

SERVES 4

2 tbsp groundnut oil or vegetable oil

1 bunch of spring onions,
roughly chopped

2.5-cm/1-inch piece fresh ginger,
finely chopped

2 lemon grass stalks, halved

2 carrots, peeled and cut into
matchsticks

1 small head broccoli, cut into florets

55 g/2 oz baby corn, halved lengthways

55 g/2 oz canned water chestnuts,
drained

1 tbsp Red Curry Paste (see page 11)

225 g/8 oz dried medium egg noodles

4 tbsp sesame seeds

salt

1. Heat the oil in a preheated wok, add the spring onions, ginger and lemon grass
   and stir-fry over a medium–high heat for 2–3 minutes, until starting to soften. Add
   the carrots, broccoli and baby corn and stir-fry for 3–4 minutes, until starting to
   soften. Add the water chestnuts and curry paste and stir well, then stir-fry for a
   further 2–3 minutes. Discard the lemon grass.

2. Meanwhile, bring a large saucepan of lightly salted water to the boil, add the
   noodles and cook for 4–5 minutes, or until just tender. Drain and return to the
   saucepan. Add the sesame seeds and toss to coat.

3. Add the noodles to the stir-fried vegetables and serve immediately.

Red Curry with Mixed Leaves

SERVES 4

2 tbsp groundnut oil or vegetable oil

2 onions, thinly sliced

1 bunch of fine asparagus spears

400 ml/14 fl oz coconut milk

2 tbsp Red Curry Paste (see page 11)

3 fresh kaffir lime leaves

225 g/8 oz baby spinach leaves

2 heads pak choi, chopped

1 small head Chinese leaves, shredded

handful of fresh coriander, chopped

freshly cooked plain rice, to serve

1. Heat a wok over a medium–high heat and add the oil. Add the onions and asparagus and stir-fry for 1–2 minutes.

2. Add the coconut milk, curry paste and lime leaves and bring gently to the boil, stirring occasionally. Add the spinach, pak choi and Chinese leaves and cook, stirring, for 2–3 minutes, until wilted. Add the coriander and stir well. Serve immediately with rice.

Spring Vegetable Rice

SERVES 4

2 tbsp groundnut oil or vegetable oil

2 shallots, chopped

2 garlic cloves, crushed

225 g/8 oz basmati rice

600 ml/1 pint chicken stock

1 tbsp Red Curry Paste (see page 11)

1 tsp Thai fish sauce

3 tbsp soy sauce

175 g/6 oz baby corn, halved lengthways

115 g/4 oz baby carrots, halved lengthways

55 g/2 oz mangetout

55 g/2 oz fresh beansprouts

4 tbsp sesame seeds

handful of fresh coriander, chopped

2 tbsp sesame oil

salt

1. Heat the oil in a preheated wok, add the shallots and garlic and stir-fry over a medium–high heat for 1–2 minutes. Add the rice and stir-fry for 2–3 minutes. Add the stock, curry paste, fish sauce and soy sauce and bring to the boil, stirring occasionally. Reduce the heat and simmer for 10–12 minutes, until the rice is tender, adding more stock or boiling water, if necessary,

2. Meanwhile, bring a saucepan of lightly salted water to the boil, add the baby corn and carrots and cook for 2–3 minutes, until just tender. Add the mangetout and cook for 1 minute. Add the beansprouts, stir well, then drain.

3. Heat a dry frying pan until hot, add the sesame seeds and cook over a medium–high heat, shaking the frying pan frequently, for 30–45 seconds, until lightly browned.

4. Add the drained vegetables, coriander and sesame oil to the rice and serve immediately, scattered with the toasted sesame seeds.

Carrot and Pumpkin Curry

SERVES 4

150 ml/5 fl oz vegetable stock

2.5-cm/1-inch piece fresh galangal, sliced

2 garlic cloves, chopped

1 lemon grass stem (white part only), finely chopped

2 fresh red chillies, deseeded and chopped

4 carrots, peeled and cut into chunks

225 g/8 oz pumpkin, peeled, deseeded and cut into cubes

2 tbsp vegetable oil or groundnut oil

2 shallots, finely chopped

3 tbsp Thai yellow curry paste

400 ml/14 fl oz coconut milk

4–6 fresh Thai basil sprigs

25 g/1 oz toasted pumpkin seeds, to garnish

1. Pour the stock into a large saucepan and bring to the boil. Add the galangal, half the garlic, the lemon grass and chillies and simmer for 5 minutes. Add the carrots and pumpkin and simmer for 5–6 minutes, until tender.

2. Heat a wok over a medium–high heat and add the oil. Add the shallots and the remaining garlic and stir-fry for 2–3 minutes. Add the curry paste and stir-fry for 1–2 minutes.

3. Stir the shallot mixture into the saucepan and add the coconut milk and basil. Simmer for 2–3 minutes. Serve hot, sprinkled with the toasted pumpkin seeds.

Tofu and Vegetable Curry

SERVES 4

2 tbsp vegetable oil or groundnut oil, plus extra for deep-frying

225 g/8 oz firm tofu, drained and cut into cubes

2 onions, chopped

2 garlic cloves, chopped

1 fresh red chilli, deseeded and sliced

3 celery sticks, sliced diagonally

225 g/8 oz mushrooms, thickly sliced

115 g/4 oz baby corn cobs, cut in half

1 red pepper, deseeded and cut into strips

3 tbsp Red Curry Paste (see page 11)

400 ml/14 fl oz coconut milk

1 tsp palm sugar or soft light brown sugar

2 tbsp Thai soy sauce

225 g/8 oz baby spinach leaves

1. Heat the oil for deep-frying in a preheated wok, deep saucepan or deep-fat fryer to 180–190°C/350–375°F, or until a cube of bread browns in 30 seconds. Add the tofu, in batches, and cook for 4–5 minutes until crisp and browned all over. Remove with a slotted spoon and drain on kitchen paper.

2. Heat the 2 tablespoons of oil in a wok or frying pan, add the onions, garlic and chilli and stir-fry for 1–2 minutes, until they start to soften. Add the celery, mushrooms, corn cobs and red pepper and stir-fry for 3–4 minutes, until soft.

3. Stir in the curry paste and coconut milk and gradually bring to the boil. Add the sugar and soy sauce and then the spinach. Cook, stirring constantly, until the spinach has wilted. Serve immediately, topped with the tofu.

Cabbage and Coconut Curry

SERVES 4–6

3 tbsp vegetable oil

1 tsp mustard seeds

1 small onion, sliced

¼ white cabbage, core removed, leaves shredded

½ small green cabbage, core removed, leaves shredded

100–125 ml/3–4 fl oz water

½ tsp white peppercorns, crushed

4 tbsp toasted coconut flakes, plus extra to garnish

3 tbsp chopped coriander leaves

juice of ½ lime

salt

SPICE PASTE

50 g/1¾ oz sachet creamed coconut, melted

1 green chilli, deseeded and roughly chopped

1 tbsp finely chopped fresh ginger

2 garlic cloves, sliced

1 small onion, finely chopped

½ tsp salt

1 tsp cumin seeds

½ tsp ground turmeric

1. Purée the spice paste ingredients in a food processor or blender, adding a splash of water to moisten.

2. Heat a wok over a medium–high heat and add the oil. Add the mustard seeds and fry until they start to crackle. Reduce the heat to medium, then add the onion and stir-fry until golden. Stir in the spice paste and fry for 30 seconds.

3. Add the shredded white cabbage and green cabbage and pour in the water, stirring well so the cabbage is covered with the paste. Season with the crushed peppercorns and a little salt. Cover and cook over a low heat for 7–10 minutes, stirring now and again to prevent sticking.

4. When the cabbage is tender, add the coconut flakes, coriander and lime juice. Stir for a minute to heat through, then serve, garnished with coconut flakes.

Peppered Beef Salad

SERVES 4

4 x 115-g/4-oz fillet steaks

2 tbsp black peppercorns, crushed

1 tsp five-spice powder

115 g/4 oz beansprouts

2.5-cm/1-inch piece fresh ginger, finely
chopped

4 shallots, finely sliced

1 red pepper, deseeded and
thinly sliced

3 tbsp Thai soy sauce

2 fresh red chillies, deseeded and sliced

½ lemon grass stalk, finely chopped

3 tbsp vegetable oil or groundnut oil

1 tbsp sesame oil

lime half, to garnish

1. Wash the steaks and pat dry on kitchen paper. Mix the peppercorns with the
   five-spice powder and press onto all sides of the steaks. Cook on a griddle pan or
   under a grill for 2–3 minutes on each side, or until cooked to your liking.

2. Meanwhile mix the beansprouts, half the ginger, the shallots and red pepper
   together and divide between four plates. Mix the remaining ginger, soy sauce,
   chillies, lemon grass, vegetable oil and sesame oil together.

3. Slice the beef and arrange on the vegetables. Drizzle with the dressing and serve
   immediately, garnished with half a lime.

Gingered Chicken and Vegetable Salad

SERVES 4

4 skinless, boneless chicken breasts

4 spring onions, chopped

2.5-cm/1-inch piece fresh ginger, finely chopped

2 garlic cloves, crushed

2 tbsp vegetable oil or groundnut oil

SALAD

1 tbsp vegetable or groundnut oil

1 onion, sliced

2 garlic cloves, chopped

115 g/4 oz baby sweetcorn, halved

115 g/4 oz mangetout, halved lengthways

1 red pepper, deseeded and sliced

7.5-cm/3-inch piece cucumber, peeled, deseeded and sliced

4 tbsp Thai soy sauce

1 tbsp jaggery or soft light brown sugar

a few Thai basil leaves

175 g/6 oz fine egg noodles

1. Cut the chicken into 2.5-cm/1-inch cubes. Mix the spring onions, ginger, garlic and oil together in a shallow dish and add the chicken. Cover and marinate for at least 3 hours. Lift the meat out of the marinade and set aside.

2. Heat the oil in a wok, add the onion and cook for 1–2 minutes. Add the garlic and the rest of the vegetables, except the cucumber, and cook for 2–3 minutes until just tender. Add the cucumber, half the soy sauce, the sugar and the basil, and mix gently.

3. Soak the noodles for 2–3 minutes (check the packet instructions), or until tender, and drain well. Sprinkle the remaining soy sauce over them and arrange on plates. Top with the cooked vegetables.

4. Add a little more oil to the wok if necessary, add the chicken and cook over a fairly high heat until browned on all sides. Arrange the chicken on top of the salad and serve hot or warm.

Red Chicken Salad

SERVES 4

4 boneless chicken breasts

2 tbsp Red Curry Paste (see page 11)

2 tbsp vegetable oil or groundnut oil

1 head Chinese leaves, shredded

175 g/6 oz pak choi, torn into
  large pieces

½ savoy cabbage, shredded

2 shallots, finely chopped

2 garlic cloves, crushed

1 tbsp rice wine vinegar

2 tbsp sweet chilli sauce

2 tbsp Thai soy sauce

1. Score the chicken several times and rub the curry paste into each cut. Cover and chill overnight.

2. When ready to cook, put the chicken in a wok over a medium heat and cook for 5–6 minutes, turning once or twice, until cooked through. Remove from the wok and keep warm.

3. Heat 1 tablespoon of the oil in the wok and stir-fry the Chinese leaves, pak choi and cabbage until just wilted. Add the remaining oil, shallots and garlic and stir-fry until just tender but not brown. Add the vinegar, chilli sauce and soy sauce. Remove from the heat.

4. Arrange the stir-fried leaves on four serving plates. Slice the chicken, arrange on top of the leaves and drizzle the hot dressing over the dish. Serve immediately.

Duck Salad

SERVES 4

4 boneless duck breasts, skin on

1 lemon grass stalk, broken into three
 and each cut in half lengthways

3 tbsp vegetable oil or groundnut oil

2 tbsp sesame oil

1 tsp Thai fish sauce

1 fresh green chilli, deseeded and
 chopped

2 tbsp Red Curry Paste (see page 11)

½ fresh pineapple, peeled and sliced

7.5-cm/3-inch piece cucumber, peeled,
 deseeded and sliced

3 tomatoes, cut into wedges

1 onion, thinly sliced

fresh coriander, to garnish

DRESSING

juice of 1 lemon

2 garlic cloves, crushed

1 tsp jaggery or soft light brown sugar

2 tbsp vegetable oil or groundnut oil

1. Unwrap the duck and let the skin dry out overnight in the refrigerator.

2. The following day, slash the skin side five or six times. Mix the lemon grass,
   2 tablespoons of the vegetable oil, all the sesame oil, fish sauce, chilli and curry
   paste together in a shallow dish and place the duck breasts in the mixture. Turn to
   coat and rub the marinade into the meat. Chill for 2–3 hours.

3. Heat the remaining oil in a wok, add the duck and cook, skin-side down, over a
   medium heat for 3–4 minutes until the skin is browned and crisp and the meat is
   cooked most of the way through. Turn over the breasts and cook until browned
   and the meat is cooked to your liking.

4. Meanwhile, arrange the pineapple, cucumber, tomatoes and onions on a platter.
   Mix the dressing ingredients together and pour over the top.

5. Lift the duck out of the wok and slice thickly. Arrange the duck slices on top of the
   salad and serve while still hot, garnished with coriander.

Sea Bass and Mango Salad

SERVES 2

2 small sea bass, cleaned

1 tbsp Red Curry Paste (see page 11)

small handful of fresh coriander, chopped

150 ml/5 fl oz coconut milk

2 tbsp sweet chilli sauce

6–8 Thai basil leaves, chopped

½ tsp Thai fish sauce

1 tsp rice wine vinegar

1 mango, stoned, peeled and sliced

selection of mixed salad leaves, to serve

1. Place the fish on a chopping board. Mix the curry paste and coriander together and stuff some of the mixture inside each fish cavity. Cover and leave to marinate for 1–2 hours.

2. Preheat the oven to 200°C/400°F/Gas Mark 6. Place the fish in a roasting tin. Mix the coconut milk, chilli sauce, basil, fish sauce and vinegar together and pour over the fish. Arrange the mango slices in the tin. Cover with foil and cook in the preheated oven for 15 minutes.

3. Remove the foil and cook the fish, uncovered, for a further 10–15 minutes until it is cooked.

4. Place the fish on two warmed serving plates, drizzle with the cooking sauces and serve with the mixed salad leaves.

Caramelized Tuna Salad

SERVES 4

175 g/6 oz fresh beansprouts

10-cm/4-inch piece cucumber

20 g/¾ oz coriander leaves

20 g/¾ oz mint leaves

1 tsp sesame oil, plus a few drops
  for drizzling

1 tbsp groundnut oil

450 g/1 lb fresh tuna, cut into
  2.5-cm/1-inch chunks

salt

2 tbsp salted roasted peanuts, crushed,
  to garnish

DRESSING

2 tsp rapeseed oil

1 tsp finely chopped fresh ginger

½–1 small red chilli, deseeded and
  finely chopped

4 tbsp light soy sauce

1 tbsp Thai fish sauce

1 tbsp tamarind paste

6 tbsp soft light brown sugar

1. To make the dressing, heat a small wok over a high heat and add the oil. Add the ginger and chilli and fry for a few seconds. Add the soy sauce, fish sauce and tamarind paste. Stir for 30 seconds, then add the sugar and stir until dissolved. Remove the wok from the heat and set aside.

2. Rinse the beansprouts in boiling water and drain. Blot dry with kitchen paper. Peel the cucumber, halve lengthways and scoop out the seeds. Thinly slice the flesh diagonally.

3. Put the beansprouts, cucumber, coriander and mint leaves in a bowl. Season with a pinch of salt and a few drops of sesame oil. Toss to combine, then divide between individual serving plates.

4. Heat a wok over a high heat, then add the groundnut oil and sesame oil. Quickly stir-fry the tuna, turning with tongs, until coloured on the outside but still slightly red in the middle. Arrange the tuna chunks on top of the salad.

5. Reheat the dressing, thinning with a spoonful of water if necessary, and pour over the tuna. Sprinkle with the crushed peanuts and serve at once.

Hot-and-sour Vegetable Salad

SERVES 4

2 tbsp vegetable oil or groundnut oil

1 tbsp chilli oil

1 onion, sliced

2.5-cm/1-inch piece fresh ginger, grated

1 small head broccoli, cut into florets

2 carrots, cut into short thin sticks

1 red pepper, deseeded and
   cut into squares

1 yellow pepper, deseeded and
   cut into strips

55 g/2 oz mangetout, trimmed
   and halved

55 g/2 oz baby corn, halved

DRESSING

2 tbsp vegetable oil or groundnut oil

1 tsp chilli oil

1 tbsp rice wine vinegar

juice of 1 lime

½ tsp Thai fish sauce

1. Heat a wok over a medium–high heat and add the vegetable oil and chilli oil. Add the onion and ginger and sauté for 1–2 minutes until they start to soften. Add the remaining vegetables and stir-fry for 2–3 minutes until they have softened slightly. Remove from the heat and set aside.

2. Mix together the dressing ingredients. Transfer the vegetables to a serving plate and drizzle the dressing over. Serve warm, or allow the flavours to develop and serve cold.

Meat

Although meat features widely in Thai cuisine, it plays a less important role than in Western cooking. In Thailand meat is often just a component of a dish containing several other ingredients, and the dish itself is one of several served at a meal. That said, there are plenty of meat-based dishes to be enjoyed, including classic curries such as Coconut Beef Curry, lip-smacking roasts, and surprisingly zesty cold dishes such as Beef with Black Pepper and Lime, a dish originating from neighbouring Malaysia.

Thailand boasts more recipes for pork than any other meat. It is cooked in every imaginable way – in snacks, soups and salads, in curries, such as Red Pork Curry with Peppers, and in kebabs and stir-fries, including Pork Stir-fry with Cashew Nuts, Lime and Mint. In northern Thailand crisp and puffy deep-fried pork skin, the Thai equivalent of pork scratchings, is very

popular and is obligatory with relishes and curries. Also irresistible, and eaten almost everywhere, is sweet crispy pork, in which sugar plays a vital role in balancing excessively hot, sharp and salty flavours, which in turn are used to counteract the greasiness of the pork.

While pork is a favourite meat throughout most of Thailand, the Muslim community in the south exclude it from the diet for religious reasons. In this area lamb and mutton are popular and beef is also eaten. With its rich distinctive flavour, lamb stands up to the spices in the typically hearty red curries, which include the creamy, coconut-flavoured Red Lamb Curry. It is also excellent with the refreshing herbal flavours that are often found in Thai cooking, as in Green Lamb Stir-fry with Noodles and Peanuts, Stir-fried Lamb with Mint and Lamb with Lime Leaves.

Masaman Curry

SERVES 4

2 tbsp groundnut oil or vegetable oil

225 g/8 oz shallots, roughly chopped

1 garlic clove, crushed

450 g/1 lb beef fillet, thickly sliced and
  cut into 2.5-cm/1-inch cubes

2 tbsp ready-made masaman
  curry paste

3 potatoes, peeled and cut into
  2.5-cm/1-inch cubes

400 ml/14 fl oz coconut milk

2 tbsp soy sauce

150 ml/5 fl oz beef stock

1 tsp palm sugar

85 g/3 oz unsalted peanuts

handful of fresh coriander, chopped

cooked rice or noodles, to serve

1. Heat the oil in a preheated wok, add the shallots and garlic and stir-fry over
   a medium–high heat for 1–2 minutes until soft. Add the beef cubes and curry
   paste and stir-fry over a high heat for 2–3 minutes until browned all over. Add
   the potatoes, coconut milk, soy sauce, stock and sugar and bring gently to the
   boil, stirring occasionally. Reduce the heat and simmer for 8–10 minutes until the
   potatoes are tender.

2. Meanwhile, heat a separate dry frying pan until hot, add the peanuts and cook
   over a medium–high heat, shaking the frying pan frequently, for 2–3 minutes until
   lightly browned. Add to the curry with the coriander and stir well. Serve hot with
   rice or noodles.

Coconut Beef Curry

SERVES 4

1 tbsp ground coriander

1 tbsp ground cumin

3 tbsp ready-made masaman
curry paste

150 ml/5 fl oz water

75 g/2¾ oz creamed coconut

450 g/1 lb beef fillet, cut into strips

400 ml/14 fl oz coconut milk

50 g/1¾ oz unsalted peanuts,
finely chopped

2 tbsp Thai fish sauce

1 tsp palm sugar or soft light
brown sugar

4 kaffir lime leaves

fresh coriander sprigs, to garnish

freshly cooked rice, to serve

1. Combine the coriander, cumin and curry paste in a bowl. Pour the water into a saucepan, add the creamed coconut and heat until it has dissolved. Add the curry paste mixture and simmer for 1 minute.

2. Add the beef and simmer for 6–8 minutes, then add the coconut milk, peanuts, fish sauce and sugar. Simmer gently for 15–20 minutes until the meat is tender.

3. Add the lime leaves and simmer for 1–2 minutes. Garnish with coriander sprigs and serve with cooked rice.

Marinated Beef with Celery

SERVES 4

500 g/1 lb 2 oz beef fillet,
   cut into thin strips

250 ml/9 fl oz vegetable oil

3 celery stalks, cut into thin strips,
   2.5 cm/1 inch long

1 red pepper, cut into thin strips

1 red chilli, deseeded and finely sliced

lime wedges, to garnish

Thai fish sauce, to serve

MARINADE

1 tsp salt

2 tbsp Thai fish sauce

1. To make the marinade, mix the salt and fish sauce in a large bowl.

2. Add the beef to the marinade and toss to coat. Cover with clingfilm and place in the refrigerator for 1 hour to marinate.

3. Heat 225 ml/8 fl oz of the oil in a wok, add the beef and deep-fry over a medium heat for 2–3 minutes until crispy. Remove the wok from the heat and, using a slotted spoon, lift out the meat and drain it on kitchen paper. Discard all but 2 tablespoons of the oil.

4. Add the remaining oil to the wok. When it is hot add the celery, red pepper and chilli and stir-fry for 1 minute. Add the beef and cook until hot.

5. Garnish with lime wedges and serve with fish sauce.

Beef with Black Pepper and Lime

SERVES 2–3

350 g/12 oz skirt steak

½ tbsp palm sugar or light brown sugar

1 tbsp black peppercorns, crushed

4 tsp soy sauce

1 fresh red bird's eye chilli, deseeded and finely chopped

½ garlic bulb, divided into cloves and crushed

2 tbsp lime juice

½ head Chinese leaves, sliced

½ red onion, thinly sliced

1½ tbsp groundnut oil

½ tsp Thai fish sauce

handful fresh mint leaves

lime wedges, to garnish

1. Pound the steak with the blunt side of a knife. Slice diagonally across the grain into thin, bite-sized pieces and place in a shallow bowl.

2. Combine the sugar, peppercorns, soy sauce, chilli, garlic and half the lime juice in a bowl, mixing well. Pour over the beef, stirring to coat. Leave to marinate for 1 hour at room temperature, or overnight in the refrigerator.

3. Arrange the Chinese leaves in a shallow serving dish. Scatter with the onion slices.

4. Heat a wok over a high heat, then add the oil. Add the meat and stir-fry for 3 minutes, then add the fish sauce and the remaining lime juice and stir-fry for a further minute.

5. Tip the beef and juices over the Chinese leaves and onion, then scatter over the mint. Garnish with lime wedges and serve immediately with rice.

Hot Beef and Coconut Curry

SERVES 4

400 ml/14 fl oz coconut milk

2 tbsp Red Curry Paste (see page 11)

2 garlic cloves, crushed

500 g/1 lb 2 oz braising steak

2 fresh kaffir lime leaves, shredded

3 tbsp lime juice

2 tbsp Thai fish sauce

1 large fresh red chilli, deseeded and
  sliced

½ tsp ground turmeric

2 tbsp chopped fresh basil leaves

2 tbsp chopped coriander leaves

salt and pepper

shredded coconut, to garnish

freshly cooked rice, to serve

1. Place the coconut milk in a large saucepan and bring to the boil. Reduce the heat and simmer gently for 10 minutes, or until it has thickened. Stir in the curry paste and garlic and simmer for a further 5 minutes.

2. Cut the beef into 2-cm/¾-inch chunks. Add to the pan and bring to the boil, stirring constantly. Reduce the heat and add the lime leaves, lime juice, fish sauce, chilli, turmeric and ½ teaspoon of salt.

3. Cover the pan and continue simmering for 20–25 minutes, or until the meat is tender, adding a little water if the sauce looks too dry.

4. Stir in the basil and coriander and season to taste with salt and pepper. Serve immediately, garnished with shredded coconut, and with rice.

Pad Thai

SERVES 4

225 g/8 oz thick dried rice noodles

2 tbsp groundnut oil or vegetable oil

4 spring onions, roughly chopped

2 garlic cloves, crushed

2 fresh red chillies, deseeded and sliced

225 g/8 oz pork fillet, trimmed and
thinly sliced

115 g/4 oz cooked peeled large prawns

juice of 1 lime

2 tbsp Thai fish sauce

2 eggs, beaten

55 g/2 oz fresh beansprouts

handful of fresh coriander, chopped

55 g/2 oz unsalted peanuts, chopped

1. Bring a large saucepan of water to the boil, add the noodles and soak, covered, for 10 minutes until just tender, or according to the packet instructions. Drain, rinse under cold running water and set aside.

2. Heat the oil in a preheated wok, add the spring onions, garlic and chillies and stir-fry over a medium–high heat for 1–2 minutes. Add the pork and stir-fry over a high heat for 1–2 minutes until browned all over.

3. Add the prawns, lime juice, fish sauce and eggs and stir-fry over a medium heat for 2–3 minutes until the eggs have set and the prawns are heated through.

4. Add the beansprouts, most of the coriander, the peanuts and the noodles and stir-fry for 30 seconds until heated through. Serve immediately, garnished with the remaining coriander.

Caramelized Belly Pork with Star Anise

SERVES 2–3

500 g/1 1b 2 oz boneless belly
  pork strips

2 tbsp soy sauce

200 g/7 oz palm sugar
  or soft light brown sugar

4 tbsp Thai fish sauce

1 tbsp oyster sauce

2 tbsp groundnut oil

3 tbsp crisp-fried onion (from a jar)
  and 2 tbsp chopped fresh coriander,
  to garnish

SPICE PASTE

3 star anise pods

1 tsp coriander seeds or chopped fresh
  coriander root

2 tsp white peppercorns

4 garlic cloves, crushed

salt

1. Trim the rind but not the fat from the pork. Place the meat in a shallow dish and
    sprinkle with the soy sauce. Cover and leave to marinate in the refrigerator for 1–24
    hours.

2. To make the spice paste dry-fry the star anise pods and coriander seeds for 2
    minutes until fragrant. Combine with the remaining spice paste ingredients, and
    grind until smooth, using a mortar and pestle.

3. Bring a saucepan of water to the boil and steam the pork over the boiling water for
    15 minutes. Reserve the liquid and allow the meat to cool. Slice into 2-cm/¾-inch
    strips, then rub in the paste.

4. Put the sugar, fish sauce and oyster sauce into a saucepan. Stir over a medium heat
    until the sugar has melted.

5. Heat a wok over a medium–high heat. Add the oil and the pork and stir-fry until the
    meat is beginning to colour. If the pork starts to stick sprinkle it with a spoonful of
    the reserved cooking liquid. Add the sugar mixture and stir for a few minutes until
    it is bubbling and caramelized, and the meat is well coated. Sprinkle with the fried
    onion and coriander, and serve at once.

Red Pork Curry with Peppers

SERVES 4

2 tbsp vegetable oil or groundnut oil

1 onion, coarsely chopped

2 garlic cloves, chopped

450 g/1 lb pork fillet, thickly sliced

1 red pepper, deseeded and
cut into squares

175 g/6 oz mushrooms, quartered

2 tbsp Red Curry Paste (see page 11)

115 g/4 oz creamed coconut, chopped

300 ml/10 fl oz pork stock or vegetable
stock

2 tbsp Thai soy sauce

4 tomatoes, peeled, deseeded and
chopped

handful of fresh coriander, chopped

1. Heat the oil in a wok or large frying pan, add the onion and garlic and cook for
   1–2 minutes until soft but not brown.

2. Add the pork slices to the wok and stir-fry for 2–3 minutes until browned all over.
   Add the red pepper, mushrooms and curry paste.

3. Dissolve the coconut in the stock and add to the wok with the soy sauce. Bring to
   the boil and simmer for 4–5 minutes until the liquid has reduced and thickened.

4. Add the tomatoes and coriander and cook for 1–2 minutes before serving.

Pork Stir-fry with Cashew Nuts, Lime and Mint

SERVES 2

280 g/10 oz pork fillet

1 tsp coriander seeds

½ tsp white peppercorns

¼ tsp salt

¼ tsp sugar

juice and finely grated rind of 1 lime

2 tbsp groundnut oil

1 tsp finely chopped fresh ginger

1 garlic clove, thinly sliced

3 spring onions, white and green parts separated, then halved lengthways and sliced into 2-cm/¾-inch pieces

1 small green pepper, deseeded and thinly sliced

2 tbsp cashew nuts, roughly chopped

large pinch of salt

1 tbsp chicken stock

1 tsp Thai fish sauce

2 tbsp roughly chopped fresh mint leaves, to garnish

1. Diagonally slice the pork across the grain into thin bite-sized pieces. Flatten with the back of a knife blade and spread out on a plate. Using a mortar and pestle, crush the coriander seeds, peppercorns, salt, sugar and lime rind together. Spread the mixture over both sides of the pork, pressing it in well. Leave to stand for 15 minutes.

2. Heat a wok over a high heat, then add 1 tablespoon of the oil. Add the pork and stir-fry for 2–3 minutes until no longer pink. Transfer to a plate with the cooking juices. Wipe the wok clean with kitchen paper.

3. Heat the wok over a medium–high heat, then add the remaining oil. Add the ginger and garlic and stir-fry for a few seconds. Add the white spring onion and green pepper and stir-fry for 2 minutes. Add the cashew nuts and salt, then stir-fry for a further minute.

4. Increase the heat to high, then return the pork and juices to the wok. Add the stock, lime juice, fish sauce and the green spring onion. Stir-fry for 30 seconds to heat through, then sprinkle with the mint and serve.

Red Roasted Pork with Peppered Noodles

SERVES 2

1 tbsp Red Curry Paste (see page 11)

2 tbsp soy sauce

350 g/12 oz piece pork fillet, trimmed

225 g/8 oz fine dried egg noodles

2 tbsp groundnut oil or vegetable oil

1 red onion, chopped

2.5-cm/1-inch piece fresh ginger, peeled and finely chopped

1 garlic clove, finely chopped

1 orange pepper, deseeded and chopped

1 red pepper, deseeded and chopped

1 tbsp pepper

1 small bunch of fresh chives, snipped

handful of fresh coriander, chopped

1. Mix the curry paste and soy sauce together in a small bowl and spread over the pork. Cover and leave to marinate in the refrigerator for 1 hour.

2. Meanwhile, preheat the oven to 200°C/400°F/Gas Mark 6. Place the pork in a roasting tin and roast in the preheated oven for 20–25 minutes until cooked through. Remove from the oven, cover with foil and leave to rest for 15 minutes.

3. Meanwhile, bring a large saucepan of water to the boil, add the noodles and cook for 4 minutes until just tender, or according to the packet instructions. Drain, rinse under cold running water and set aside.

4. Heat the oil in a preheated wok, add the onion, ginger and garlic and stir-fry over a medium–high heat for 1–2 minutes. Add the orange pepper and red pepper, season with the tablespoon of pepper and stir-fry for 2–3 minutes until tender. Stir in the chives and most of the coriander.

5. Add the drained noodles to the pepper mixture and toss together until well mixed. Divide between two serving dishes. Slice the pork and arrange it on top of the noodles. Scatter with the remaining coriander and serve immediately.

Minced Pork Kebabs with Sweet Chilli Dipping Sauce

SERVES 4

1 large onion, chopped

2 garlic cloves, crushed

450 g/1 lb minced pork

1 tsp salt

2 tbsp sweet chilli dipping sauce,
  plus extra to serve

handful of fresh coriander, chopped,
  plus extra sprigs to garnish (optional)

1 egg

egg-fried rice, to serve

1. Put all the ingredients except the rice in a food processor and process to a thick paste.

2. Divide the pork mixture into eight portions. Using damp hands, squeeze one portion evenly around a flat metal skewer to make eight kebabs. Cover and chill in the refrigerator for at least 1 hour.

3. Heat a ridged griddle pan over a medium–high heat, add the kebabs and cook, turning occasionally, for 5–6 minutes until browned all over and cooked through. Serve immediately on a bed of egg-fried rice with sweet chilli dipping sauce, garnished with sprigs of fresh coriander, if using.

Green Lamb Stir-fry with Noodles and Peanuts

SERVES 4

450 g/1 lb boneless lamb

2 tbsp soy sauce

2 tsp cornflour

200 ml/7 fl oz chicken stock

1 tbsp Thai fish sauce

100 g/3½ oz Chinese garlic chives,
   or green stalks from 2 bunches of
   spring onions

125 g/4½ oz dried egg noodles

3 tbsp groundnut oil

2-cm/¾-inch piece galangal or fresh
   ginger, finely chopped

5 tbsp Green Curry Paste
   (see page 11)

50 g/1¾ oz dry-roasted peanuts,
   roughly chopped

juice of ½ lime

salt

lime slices, to serve

1. Slice the lamb into 4 x 1-cm/1½ x ½-inch strips and put in a shallow dish. Sprinkle with the soy sauce, cornflour and a pinch of salt, tossing well to coat. Cover and leave to marinate in the refrigerator for 1–24 hours.

2. Combine the stock, fish sauce and ½ teaspoon of salt. Trim the garlic chives and slice into 2-cm/¾-inch lengths.

3. Cook the noodles according to the packet instructions. Drain, return to the pan, and toss with 1 tablespoon of the oil.

4. Heat a wok over a high heat. Add the remaining oil and stir-fry the lamb for 3 minutes or until no longer pink. Add the galangal and curry paste and stir for another minute. Pour in the stock mixture and stir until boiling. Add the noodles, tossing to coat with the sauce. Add the chives and stir-fry for a few seconds until wilted. Sprinkle with the peanuts and lime juice, and serve at once with lime slices.

Red Lamb Curry

SERVES 4

2 tbsp vegetable oil

1 large onion, sliced

2 garlic cloves, crushed

500 g/1 lb 2 oz lean boneless leg of lamb, cut into 3-cm/1¼-inch cubes

2 tbsp Red Curry Paste (see page 11)

150 ml/5 fl oz coconut milk

1 tbsp soft light brown sugar

1 large red pepper, deseeded and thickly sliced

150 ml/5 fl oz lamb stock or beef stock

1 tbsp Thai fish sauce

2 tbsp lime juice

225 g/8 oz canned water chestnuts, drained

2 tbsp chopped fresh coriander

2 tbsp chopped fresh basil, plus extra leaves to garnish

salt and pepper

1. Heat a wok over a high heat, then add the oil. Add the onion and garlic and stir-fry for 2–3 minutes until soft. Add the lamb and stir-fry quickly until lightly browned.

2. Stir in the curry paste and cook for a few seconds, then add the coconut milk and sugar and bring to the boil. Reduce the heat and leave to simmer for 15 minutes, stirring occasionally.

3. Stir in the red pepper, stock, fish sauce and lime juice, then cover and simmer for a further 15 minutes, or until the lamb is tender.

4. Add the water chestnuts, coriander and chopped basil and season to taste with salt and pepper. Transfer to serving plates, then garnish with basil leaves and serve immediately.

Lamb with Lime Leaves

SERVES 4

450 g/1 lb lean boneless lamb
  (leg or loin fillet)

2 tbsp groundnut oil

2 fresh bird's eye chillies, deseeded and
  finely chopped

2 garlic cloves, crushed

4 shallots, chopped

2 lemon grass stems, sliced

6 fresh kaffir lime leaves

1 tbsp tamarind paste

2 tbsp palm sugar or soft light
  brown sugar

300 ml/10 fl oz coconut milk

175 g/6 oz cherry tomatoes, halved

1 tbsp chopped fresh coriander

freshly cooked Thai fragrant rice,
  to serve

1. Using a sharp knife, cut the lamb into thin strips or cubes. Heat a wok over a high heat, then add the oil. Add the chillies, garlic, shallots, lemon grass, kaffir lime leaves, tamarind paste and sugar.

2. Add the lamb to the wok and stir-fry for 5 minutes, tossing well so that the meat is evenly coated in the spice mixture.

3. Pour the coconut milk into the wok and bring to the boil. Reduce the heat and simmer for 20 minutes.

4. Add the cherry tomatoes and chopped coriander to the wok and simmer for 5 minutes. Transfer to serving plates and serve with rice.

Stir-fried Lamb with Mint

SERVES 4

2 tbsp vegetable oil

2 garlic cloves, finely sliced

2 fresh red chillies, deseeded and cut
  into thin strips

1 onion, thinly sliced

1½ tbsp Madras curry paste

500 g/1 lb 2 oz lamb fillet,
  cut into thin strips

225 g/8 oz canned baby corn, drained

4 spring onions, finely chopped

55 g/2 oz fresh mint leaves, coarsely
  shredded

1 tbsp Thai fish sauce

freshly cooked rice, to serve

1. Heat half the oil in a preheated wok or large frying pan. Add the garlic and chillies
   and cook until soft. Remove and reserve. Add the onion and cook for 5 minutes,
   or until soft. Remove and reserve.

2. Heat the remaining oil in the wok. Add the curry paste and cook for 1 minute.
   Add the lamb, in batches if necessary, and cook for 5–8 minutes, or until cooked
   through and tender.

3. Return the onion to the wok with the baby corn, spring onions, mint leaves and fish
   sauce. Cook until heated through. Sprinkle the garlic and chillies over and serve
   with rice.

Poultry

A universal favourite and infinitely adaptable, chicken shows up in the myriad dishes on the Thai menu. It was once native to the South-East Asian jungle and wild birds still exist. Mildly flavoured and juicy, chicken is the perfect meat for a wide range of dishes, not only the classic fiery red, green and yellow curries, but also the milder-flavoured Chicken with Vegetables and Coriander Rice.

There are also countless duck dishes, many emanating from China, where duck was domesticated many centuries ago. With its satisfyingly rich, sweet meaty flavour, duck not only goes well with salty and sour foods, it also stands up well to the highly incendiary heat of chillies, as in Duck Jungle Curry, and is also delicious in more subtle dishes, such as Duck with Chilli Jam and Deep-fried Shallots. For a special occasion try the mouthwatering Crispy Roast Duck with Pickled Plums.

Turkey sometimes appears on the menu, especially in the central region of the country, but it is generally not popular with home cooks because it is too large to be practical and the flesh can sometimes be dry and dense. However, in the West, where turkey is sold in portions, it can be used in curries and stir-fries in the same way as chicken. It also makes a good substitute for pork as the flesh has a similar texture.

With the Thai insistence on freshness, poultry is always freshly killed and sold with head and feet intact, or, as an absolute guarantee of freshness, it is purchased live. It is obviously not practical for Western cooks to keep live fowl, but it is worth buying the best quality you can afford.

Green Chicken Curry

SERVES 4

2 tbsp groundnut oil or sunflower oil

2 tbsp Green Curry Paste (see page 11)

500 g/1 lb 2 oz skinless, boneless chicken breasts, cut into cubes

2 kaffir lime leaves, roughly torn

1 lemon grass stalk, finely chopped

225 ml/8 fl oz coconut milk

16 baby aubergines, halved

2 tbsp Thai fish sauce

fresh Thai basil sprigs and thinly sliced kaffir lime leaves, to garnish

1. Heat the oil in a preheated wok or large, heavy-based frying pan. Add the curry paste and stir-fry briefly until all the aromas are released.

2. Add the chicken, lime leaves and lemon grass and stir-fry for 3–4 minutes, until the meat is beginning to colour. Add the coconut milk and aubergines and simmer gently for 8–10 minutes, or until tender.

3. Stir in the fish sauce and serve immediately, garnished with basil sprigs and sliced lime leaves.

Red Chicken Curry

SERVES 2–4

6 garlic cloves, chopped

2 red chillies, chopped

2 tbsp chopped lemon grass

1 tsp finely grated lime rind

1 tbsp chopped lime leaves

1 tbsp Red Curry Paste (see page 11)

1 tbsp coriander seeds

1 tbsp chilli oil

4 skinless, boneless chicken breasts, sliced

300 ml/10 fl oz coconut milk

300 ml/10 fl oz chicken stock

1 tbsp soy sauce

55 g/2 oz ground peanuts

3 spring onions, sliced

1 red pepper, deseeded and sliced

1 large aubergine, sliced

chopped fresh coriander, to garnish

freshly cooked rice, to serve

1. Place the garlic, chillies, lemon grass, lime rind, lime leaves, curry paste and coriander seeds in a food processor and process until the mixture is smooth.

2. Heat the oil in a preheated wok or large frying pan over a high heat. Add the chicken and the garlic mixture and stir-fry for 5 minutes. Add the coconut milk, stock and soy sauce and bring to the boil. Reduce the heat and cook, stirring, for a further 3 minutes. Stir in the ground peanuts and simmer for 20 minutes.

3. Add the spring onions, red pepper and aubergine and leave to simmer, stirring occasionally, for a further 10 minutes. Garnish with coriander and serve with cooked rice.

Yellow Chicken Curry

SERVES 4

2 tbsp vegetable oil or groundnut oil

2 onions, cut into thin wedges

2 garlic cloves, finely chopped

2 skinless, boneless chicken breasts,
  cut into strips

175 g/6 oz baby corn, halved
  lengthways

SPICE PASTE

6 tbsp Thai yellow curry paste

150 ml/5 fl oz natural yogurt

400 ml/14 fl oz water

handful of fresh coriander, chopped,
  plus extra to garnish

handful of fresh Thai basil leaves,
  shredded, plus extra sprigs to garnish

1. To make the spice paste, stir-fry the curry paste in a wok for 2–3 minutes, then stir
   in the yogurt, water and herbs. Bring to the boil, then simmer for 2–3 minutes.

2. Meanwhile, heat the oil in a wok and stir-fry the onions and garlic for 2–3 minutes.
   Add the chicken and baby corn and stir-fry for 3–4 minutes until the meat and corn
   are tender.

3. Stir in the spice paste and bring to the boil. Simmer for 2–3 minutes, until heated
   through. Serve immediately, garnished with basil sprigs.

Thai Chicken

SERVES 4

6 garlic cloves, coarsely chopped
1 tsp pepper
8 chicken legs
1 tbsp Thai fish sauce
4 tbsp dark soy sauce
fresh ginger, cut into matchsticks,
    to garnish

1. Put the garlic in a mortar, add the pepper and pound to a paste with a pestle. Using a sharp knife, make 3–4 diagonal slashes on both sides of the chicken legs. Spread the garlic paste over the chicken legs and place them in a dish. Add the fish sauce and soy sauce and turn the chicken to coat well. Cover with clingfilm and leave to marinate in the refrigerator for 2 hours.

2. Preheat the grill to medium–high. Drain the chicken legs, reserving the marinade. Put them on a grill rack and cook under the grill, turning and basting frequently with the reserved marinade, for 20–25 minutes, or until cooked through and tender. The juices should run clear when a skewer is inserted into the thickest part of the meat. Serve immediately, garnished with the ginger.

Chicken with Vegetables and Coriander Rice

SERVES 4

3 tbsp vegetable oil or groundnut oil

2 red onions, 1 chopped and 1 sliced

2 garlic cloves, chopped

2.5-cm/1-inch piece fresh ginger, peeled and chopped

2 skinless, boneless chicken breasts, cut into strips

115 g/4 oz white mushrooms

400 ml/14 oz coconut milk

55 g/2 oz mangetout

1 tbsp Thai fish sauce

2 tbsp Thai soy sauce

350 g/12 oz rice, cooked and cooled

250 g/8 oz pak choi, torn into large pieces

handful of fresh coriander, chopped

1. Heat 2 tablespoons of the oil in a wok or large frying pan, add the chopped onion, garlic and ginger and sauté together for 1–2 minutes.

2. Add the chicken and mushrooms and cook over a high heat until browned. Add the coconut milk, mangetout, fish sauce and 1 tablespoon of the soy sauce and bring to the boil. Simmer gently for 4–5 minutes until tender.

3. Meanwhile, heat the remaining oil in a separate wok or large frying pan, add the sliced onion and cook until soft but not brown.

4. Add the cooked rice, pak choi and coriander and heat through gently until the leaves have wilted and the rice is hot. Sprinkle over the remaining soy sauce and serve immediately with the chicken.

Ginger Chicken with Noodles

SERVES 4

2 tbsp vegetable oil or groundnut oil

1 onion, sliced

2 garlic cloves, finely chopped

5-cm/2-inch piece fresh ginger, thinly sliced

2 carrots, thinly sliced

4 skinless, boneless chicken breasts, cut into cubes

300 ml/10 fl oz chicken stock

4 tbsp Thai soy sauce

225 g/8 oz canned bamboo shoots, drained and rinsed

75 g/2¾ oz flat rice noodles

4 chopped spring onions and 4 tbsp chopped fresh coriander, to garnish

1. Heat the oil in a wok and stir-fry the onion, garlic, ginger and carrots for 1–2 minutes until soft. Add the chicken and stir-fry for 3–4 minutes, until the chicken is cooked through and lightly browned.

2. Add the stock, soy sauce and bamboo shoots and gradually bring to the boil. Simmer for 2–3 minutes. Meanwhile, bring a saucepan of water to the boil, add the noodles and soak for 6–8 minutes. Drain well, then garnish with the spring onions and coriander and serve immediately with the chicken stir-fry.

Chicken Curry with Fried Noodles

SERVES 4

2 tbsp groundnut oil or vegetable oil, plus extra for deep-frying

4 skinless, boneless chicken breasts, about 115 g/4 oz each, cut into 2.5-cm/1-inch cubes

2 red onions, roughly chopped

5 spring onions, roughly chopped

2 garlic cloves, finely chopped

1 fresh green chilli, deseeded and finely chopped

175 g/6 oz shiitake mushrooms, thickly sliced

2 tbsp Green Curry Paste (see page 11)

400 ml/14 fl oz coconut milk

300 ml/10 fl oz chicken stock

2 fresh kaffir lime leaves

handful of fresh coriander, chopped

handful of fresh chives, snipped

25 g/1 oz dried thin rice noodles

1. Heat the oil in a preheated wok, add the chicken, in batches, and stir-fry over a medium–high heat for 3–4 minutes until lightly browned all over. Remove with a slotted spoon, transfer to a plate and set aside.

2. Add the red onions, spring onions, garlic and chilli to the wok and stir-fry over a medium heat, adding a little more oil if necessary, for 2–3 minutes until soft but not brown. Add the mushrooms and stir-fry over a high heat for 30 seconds. Return the chicken to the wok.

3. Add the curry paste, coconut milk, stock and lime leaves and bring gently to the boil, stirring occasionally. Reduce the heat and simmer gently for 4–5 minutes until the chicken is tender and cooked through. Stir in the coriander and chives.

4. Meanwhile, heat the oil for deep-frying in a separate wok or deep-sided frying pan to 180–190°C/350–375°F, or until a cube of bread browns in 30 seconds. Divide the noodles into four portions and cook, one portion at a time, for about 2 seconds, until puffed up and crisp. Remove with a slotted spoon and drain on kitchen paper.

5. Serve the curry topped with the crispy noodles.

Seven-spice Chicken with Courgettes

SERVES 4

1 tbsp groundnut oil

1 clove garlic, finely chopped

2.5 cm/1 in piece fresh ginger, peeled and finely chopped

1 small fresh red chilli, seeded and finely chopped

350 g/12 oz skinless boneless chicken breasts, cut into thin strips

1 tbsp seven-spice powder

1 red pepper, deseeded and sliced

1 yellow pepper, deseeded and sliced

2 courgettes, thinly sliced

227 g/8 oz canned bamboo shoots, drained

2 tbsp dry sherry or apple juice

1 tbsp light soy sauce

2 tbsp chopped fresh coriander, plus extra to garnish

salt and pepper

1. Heat the oil in a non-stick wok or large frying pan. Add the garlic, ginger and chilli and stir-fry for 30 seconds to release the flavours.

2. Add the chicken and seven-spice powder and stir-fry for about 4 minutes, or until the chicken has coloured all over. Add the red pepper, yellow pepper and courgettes and stir-fry for 1–2 minutes, or until slightly soft.

3. Stir in the bamboo shoots and stir-fry for a further 2–3 minutes, or until the chicken is cooked through and tender. Add the sherry and soy sauce, season to taste with salt and pepper and sizzle for 1–2 minutes.

4. Stir in the coriander and serve immediately, garnished with extra coriander.

Chicken and Peanut Curry

SERVES 4

1 tbsp vegetable oil or groundnut oil

2 red onions, sliced

2 tbsp Penang curry paste

400 ml/14 fl oz coconut milk

150 ml/5 fl oz chicken stock

4 kaffir lime leaves, roughly torn

1 lemon grass stem, finely chopped

6 skinless, boneless chicken thighs, chopped

1 tbsp Thai fish sauce

2 tbsp Thai soy sauce

1 tsp palm sugar or soft light brown sugar

50 g/1¾ oz unsalted roasted peanuts, chopped, plus extra to serve

175 g/6 oz fresh pineapple, coarsely chopped

15-cm/6-inch piece cucumber, peeled, deseeded and thickly sliced, plus extra to serve

1. Heat a wok over a medium–high heat, then add the oil. Add the onions and stir-fry for 1 minute. Add the curry paste and stir-fry for 1–2 minutes.

2. Pour in the coconut milk and stock. Add the lime leaves and lemon grass and simmer for 1 minute. Add the chicken and gradually bring to the boil. Simmer for 8–10 minutes until the chicken is tender.

3. Stir in the fish sauce, soy sauce and sugar and simmer for 1–2 minutes. Stir in the peanuts, pineapple and cucumber and cook for 30 seconds. Serve immediately with peanuts and cucumber on top.

Shredded Chicken and Mixed Mushrooms

SERVES 4

2 tbsp vegetable oil or groundnut oil

2 skinless, boneless chicken breasts

1 red onion, sliced

2 garlic cloves, finely chopped

2.5-cm/1-inch piece fresh ginger, grated

115 g/4 oz baby button mushrooms

115 g/4 oz shiitake mushrooms, halved

115 g/4 oz chestnut mushrooms, sliced

2–3 tbsp Green Curry Paste (see page 11)

2 tbsp Thai soy sauce

4 tbsp chopped fresh parsley

cooked noodles or rice, to serve

1. Heat the oil in a wok, add the chicken and cook on all sides, until lightly browned and cooked through. Remove with a slotted spoon, shred into even-sized pieces and set aside.

2. Pour off any excess oil, then add the onion, garlic and ginger to the wok and stir-fry for 1–2 minutes, until soft. Add the mushrooms and stir-fry for 2–3 minutes, until they start to brown.

3. Add the curry paste, soy sauce and shredded chicken to the wok and stir-fry for 1–2 minutes. Stir in the parsley and serve immediately with noodles.

Crisp-fried Spicy Turkey

SERVES 3–4

450 g/1 lb turkey steaks

2 tbsp Thai fish sauce

2 tbsp light soy sauce

groundnut oil, for frying

40 g/1½ oz peanuts, roughly chopped

4 tbsp chopped Thai basil and lime
   wedges, to garnish

SPICE PASTE

2 tsp coriander seeds

1 tsp cumin seeds

2 tsp white peppercorns

seeds from 3 green cardamom pods

1 tsp sugar

1–2 fresh red chillies, deseeded and
   finely chopped

2 garlic cloves, finely chopped

1. To make the spice paste, dry-fry the coriander seeds over a medium–high heat,
   shaking the pan frequently, for 2 minutes until starting to pop. Dry-fry the cumin
   seeds for 30 seconds until fragrant, taking care not to let them burn. Grind the
   seeds to a paste with the remaining ingredients, using a mortar and pestle.

2. Pound the turkey steaks with a mallet until they are 5 mm/¼ inch thick. Slice across
   the grain into 5-mm x 4-cm/¼ x 1½-inch strips, and put in a shallow bowl. Rub the
   spice paste into the meat. Add the fish sauce and soy sauce, tossing to coat. Leave
   to marinate at room temperature for 20 minutes.

3. Heat a large wok over a high heat and add enough oil to come to a depth of
   2.5 cm/1 inch. Add the turkey and any spice paste from the bowl. Fry for
   4 minutes, turning with tongs, until beginning to colour. Add the peanuts and fry
   for a further minute, or until the turkey is crisp and golden at the edges.

4. Remove with a slotted spoon and drain on kitchen paper. Tip into a warmed
   serving dish and sprinkle with the basil. Garnish with lime wedges and serve.

Duck Jungle Curry

SERVES 4

2 tbsp groundnut oil

6 tbsp Green Curry Paste
(see page 11)

1 tbsp finely chopped galangal or
fresh ginger

4 tbsp finely chopped shallots

2 tbsp Thai fish sauce

500 ml/18 fl oz chicken stock

350 g/12 oz boneless, skinless duck
meat, thinly sliced into small strips

150 g/5½ oz Thai pea aubergines

2 small yellow courgettes, thickly sliced
diagonally

225 g/8 oz canned sliced bamboo
shoots, drained and rinsed

juice of 1 lime

handful of Thai basil leaves

freshly cooked rice, to serve

1. Heat a wok over a medium–high heat and add the oil. Add the curry paste, galangal and shallots and stir-fry for 1 minute until fragrant. Add the fish sauce and stock and bring to the boil.

2. Add the duck, aubergines and courgettes and simmer for about 3 minutes until the vegetables have softened slightly. Add the remaining ingredients and simmer for a few more minutes until the duck is tender and serve with rice.

Duck with Chilli Jam and Deep-fried Shallots

SERVES 2–4

2 Barbary duck breasts, weighing about 500 g/1 lb 2 oz in total

2 tbsp light soy sauce

3 tbsp Thai fish sauce

2 tsp groundnut oil

3 garlic cloves, very finely chopped

2-cm/¾-inch piece galangal or fresh ginger, very finely chopped

½–1 small fresh red chilli, deseeded and thinly sliced

3 tbsp chilli jam

6 tbsp chopped fresh coriander

pepper

freshly cooked rice, to serve

DEEP-FRIED SHALLOTS

125 g/4½ oz shallots, thinly sliced lengthways

groundnut oil, for deep-frying

1. Slice the duck breasts crossways into thin strips. Place in a shallow bowl in a single layer. Sprinkle with the soy sauce and 2 tablespoons of the fish sauce. Toss to coat, then cover and leave in the refrigerator for 2–24 hours, turning once.

2. To make the deep-fried shallots, heat a large wok over a high heat and add enough oil to come to a depth of 2.5 cm/1 inch. Add the shallots and fry for 8–10 minutes, turning with tongs, until golden. Be careful not to let them burn. Remove with tongs and drain on a tray covered with kitchen paper. The shallots will become crisp as they cool. Pour off the oil (keep for another use) and wipe out the wok.

3. Heat the clean wok over a high heat and add the 2 teaspoons of oil. Add the duck and marinade, garlic, galangal and chilli and stir-fry for 3 minutes.

4. Reduce the heat to medium–high and stir in the chilli jam, the remaining fish sauce and the deep-fried shallots. Season with pepper and stir-fry for 2 minutes, moistening with a little water if necessary, until the sauce is well amalgamated. Sprinkle with the coriander and serve.

Stir-fry with Duck and Peas

SERVES 4

450 g/1 lb skinless, boneless duck
   breasts

3 tbsp groundnut oil

6 large spring onions, white and green
   parts separated, diagonally sliced
   into 2-cm/¾-inch pieces

1 tsp finely chopped fresh ginger

300 g/10½ oz mangetout, halved
   diagonally

140 g/5 oz shelled peas

3 tbsp whole almonds with skin,
   halved lengthways

55 g/2 oz fresh beansprouts

freshly cooked noodles, to serve

MARINADE

1 tbsp soft light brown sugar

3 tbsp warm water

1–2 fresh red chillies, deseeded and
   very finely chopped

1 tbsp soy sauce

1 tsp Thai fish sauce

3 tbsp lime juice

1. Combine the marinade ingredients in a bowl, stirring to dissolve the sugar. Slice the duck into bite-sized pieces and add to the marinade. Leave to stand at room temperature for 30 minutes, or overnight in the refrigerator.

2. Heat a wok over a high heat, then add the oil. Add the white spring onion and the ginger and stir-fry for a few seconds. Add the duck and the marinade, and stir-fry for about 5 minutes. When the liquid has reduced slightly, add the mangetout and peas and stir-fry for a further 2–3 minutes.

3. Add the almonds, beansprouts and green spring onion, and stir-fry for a few seconds to heat through. Serve with noodles.

Duck with Mixed Peppers

SERVES 4

1 tbsp vegetable oil or groundnut oil

2 duck breasts, skin on

1 onion, sliced

2 garlic cloves, chopped

1 red pepper, deseeded and chopped

1 green pepper, deseeded and chopped

1 yellow pepper, deseeded and chopped

4 tomatoes, peeled, deseeded and chopped

150 ml/5 fl oz chicken stock

3 tbsp Thai soy sauce

cooked noodles, garnished with chopped onion, to serve

1. Heat the oil in a wok and cook the duck breasts over a high heat until crisp and browned. Turn over and cook until cooked through. Lift out and keep warm.

2. Pour off any excess fat, add the onion and garlic and stir-fry for 2–3 minutes until soft and lightly browned.

3. Add the red pepper, green pepper and yellow pepper and stir-fry for 2–3 minutes until tender. Add the tomatoes, stock and soy sauce and simmer for 1–2 minutes. Transfer to a serving plate. Slice the duck thickly and arrange on top, spooning any sauce over it. Serve with freshly cooked noodles garnished with chopped onion.

Crispy Roast Duck and Pickled Plums

SERVES 4

4 boneless duck breasts, about
175 g/6 oz each

3 spring onions, finely chopped

2 garlic cloves, finely chopped

4 tbsp oyster sauce

1 tbsp groundnut oil or vegetable oil

freshly cooked noodles, to serve

PICKLED PLUMS

55 g/2 oz caster sugar

4 tbsp white wine vinegar

1 fresh red chilli, deseeded and finely
chopped

½ tsp salt

4 plums, stoned and quartered

1. Use a sharp knife to make diagonal slashes in both directions in the skin of the duck breasts. Mix the spring onions, garlic and oyster sauce together in a small bowl and spread over the duck skin. Cover and leave to marinate in the refrigerator for 1 hour.

2. Meanwhile, to make the pickled plums, put all the ingredients except the plums in a saucepan, place over a low heat and simmer gently for 10–15 minutes. Add the plums and simmer for a further 5 minutes until just starting to soften. Leave to cool.

3. Preheat the oven to 200°C/400°F/Gas Mark 6. Heat the oil in a large frying pan, add the duck breasts, skin-side down, and cook for 2–3 minutes until browned. Turn over and cook on the other side for 1–2 minutes.

4. Transfer the duck breasts to a roasting tin and roast in the preheated oven for 10–15 minutes until just cooked through. Remove from the oven, cover with foil and leave to rest for 10 minutes.

5. Serve the duck breasts with the pickled plums, noodles and stir-fried vegetables, if using.

Fish and Seafood

With more than 1,500 miles/2,500 km of coastline and extensive inland waterways, Thailand boasts more fish and shellfish dishes than any based on meat or poultry. Vast areas of the daily markets are given over to freshwater and sea fish and to every imaginable type of shellfish, ranging from succulent lobsters and crayfish, clams and scallops, to cockles and mussels, tiny shrimp and giant freshwater prawns. Furthermore, almost all Thai dishes are seasoned with fish sauce or shrimp paste, or both.

Flavoursome oily fish, such as mackerel and tuna, are popular, as are dense-fleshed swordfish and barramundi. The flesh of these fish is juicy and firm enough to use for kebabs and curries, while the meaty flavors hold their own with chillies and robust spices.

Deep-fried fish is also popular. Thai cooks do their deep-frying in less oil, at a lower heat and for longer than we do in the West. The technique produces wonderfully golden, crisp and almost chewy pieces of fish that are heavenly alongside a contrastingly creamy coconut fish curry.

One of the tastiest ways of cooking a whole fish is to wrap it in banana leaves or foil – a good example of this is Steamed Sea Bream with Ginger. The fish cooks in its own juices, which are permeated with zesty spices, lime juice and salty fish sauce.

Freshness is paramount, so fish are kept alive in tanks and buckets until purchased, and small shellfish are sold in leak-proof polythene bags – no self-respecting Thai cook would dream of buying anything else.

Green Fish Curry

SERVES 4

2 tbsp vegetable oil

1 garlic clove, chopped

2 tbsp Green Curry Paste (see page 11)

1 small aubergine, diced

125 ml/4 fl oz coconut milk

2 tbsp Thai fish sauce

1 tsp sugar

225 g/8 oz firm white fish fillets, cut into pieces

125 ml/4 fl oz fish stock

2 kaffir lime leaves, finely shredded

about 15 fresh Thai basil leaves

sprigs of fresh dill, to garnish

1. Heat the oil in a large frying pan or preheated wok over a medium heat until almost smoking. Add the garlic and cook until golden. Add the curry paste and stir-fry for a few seconds before adding the aubergine. Stir-fry for about 4–5 minutes until soft.

2. Add the coconut milk, bring to the boil and stir until it thickens and curdles slightly. Add the fish sauce and sugar and stir well.

3. Add the fish pieces and stock. Simmer for 3–4 minutes, stirring occasionally, until the fish is just tender. Add the lime leaves and basil, then cook for a further minute. Transfer to a warmed serving dish, garnish with a few sprigs of fresh dill and serve at once.

Fish Curry with Rice Noodles

SERVES 4

2 tbsp vegetable oil or groundnut oil

1 large onion, chopped

2 garlic cloves, chopped

85 g/3 oz button mushrooms

225 g/8 oz monkfish, cut into 2.5-cm/1-inch cubes

225 g/8 oz salmon fillets, cut into 2.5-cm/1-inch cubes

225 g/8 oz cod, cut into 2.5-cm/1-inch cubes

2 tbsp Red Curry Paste (see page 11)

400 ml/14 fl oz coconut milk

handful of fresh coriander, chopped, plus extra to garnish

1 tsp palm sugar or soft light brown sugar

1 tsp Thai fish sauce

115 g/4 oz rice noodles

3 spring onions, chopped

55 g/2 oz beansprouts

a few fresh Thai basil leaves

1. Heat the oil in a wok or large frying pan, add the onion, garlic and mushrooms and fry gently until soft but not brown.

2. Add the fish, curry paste and coconut milk and bring gently to the boil. Simmer for 2–3 minutes before adding the coriander, sugar and fish sauce. Keep warm.

3. Meanwhile, soak the noodles for 3–4 minutes (or according to the packet instructions) or until tender and drain well through a colander. Put the colander and noodles over a saucepan of simmering water. Add the spring onions, beansprouts and basil and steam on top of the noodles for 1–2 minutes, or until just wilted.

4. Pile the noodles into warmed serving dishes, top with the fish curry and serve immediately, garnished with coriander.

Mixed Fish and Coconut Curry

SERVES 4

2 tbsp groundnut oil or vegetable oil

6 spring onions, cut into
2.5-cm/1-inch lengths

1 large carrot, peeled and cut into
matchsticks

55 g/2 oz French beans, trimmed and
cut into short lengths

2 tbsp Red Curry Paste (see page 11)

700 ml/1¼ pints coconut milk

225 g/8 oz skinned white fish fillet,
such as cod or coley, cut into
2.5-cm/1-inch cubes

225 g/8 oz squid, cleaned and cut into
thick rings

225 g/8 oz large raw prawns, peeled
and deveined

55 g/2 oz fresh beansprouts

115 g/4 oz dried rice noodles, cooked
according to the packet instructions
and drained

handful of fresh coriander, chopped

handful of fresh Thai basil leaves,
to garnish

1. Heat the oil in a preheated wok, add the spring onions, carrot and beans and
   stir-fry over a medium–high heat for 2–3 minutes until starting to soften.

2. Stir in the curry paste, then add the coconut milk. Bring gently to the boil, stirring
   occasionally, then reduce the heat and simmer for 2–3 minutes. Add all the seafood
   and beansprouts and simmer for 2–3 minutes until just cooked through and the
   prawns have turned pink.

3. Stir in the cooked noodles and coriander and cook for 1 minute. Serve the curry
   immediately, scattered with the Thai basil.

Monkfish Kebabs with Red Peppers and Prawns

SERVES 4

2 red peppers, deseeded and cut
   lengthways into 6 wedges

350 g/12 oz monkfish tail

juice of ½ lime

1 tsp Red Curry Paste (see page 11)

handful of fresh coriander, chopped,
   plus a few sprigs to garnish

225 g/8 oz raw shell-on king or tiger
   prawns

freshly cooked rice, to serve

1. Preheat the grill to high. Soak 12 bamboo skewers in cold water for at least 30 minutes. Meanwhile, arrange the red pepper wedges, skin-side up, on a baking sheet and cook under the preheated grill for 5–8 minutes until the skin is blackened. Leave to cool, then peel off the skin. Cut the flesh into 2.5-cm/1-inch squares.

2. Peel the grey membrane off the monkfish and discard. Cut down either side of the central bone to make two long pieces of fish. Cut into 2.5-cm/1-inch cubes.

3. Mix the lime juice, curry paste and coriander together in a large bowl. Add the fish cubes and toss to coat in the mixture. Thread the red pepper wedges, monkfish and prawns alternately on to the bamboo skewers. Cover and leave to marinate in the refrigerator for 30 minutes.

4. Cook the kebabs in a preheated ridged griddle pan over a medium–high heat, turning occasionally, for 4–5 minutes until browned all over and cooked through. Serve immediately, garnished with coriander, and with rice.

Swordfish Kebabs

SERVES 4

700 g/1 lb 9 oz swordfish steaks,
  cut into bite-sized chunks
2 red peppers, deseeded and cut into
  bite-sized squares
1 red onion, cut into bite-sized chunks
2 limes
2 garlic cloves, finely chopped
2 tsp chopped fresh ginger

2 fresh red chillies, deseeded and finely
  chopped
1 tsp dried lemon grass
2 tbsp sesame oil
1 handful of fresh coriander leaves,
  chopped
lime wedges, to garnish

1. Put the swordfish, red peppers and onion into a non-metallic dish. Finely grate the
    rind (without pith) from one of the limes and add to the dish, then squeeze the
    juice from both limes and add to the dish along with all the remaining ingredients.
    Stir well, cover and leave to marinate in a cool place for 30 minutes–1 hour,
    if possible.

2. Preheat the grill to high or preheat the barbecue. Thread the swordfish, red
    peppers and onion alternately onto four metal or pre-soaked wooden skewers.
    Cook the kebabs under the grill for 8 minutes, turning halfway through and
    spooning over any remaining marinade as you do so. Serve immediately, garnished
    with lime wedges.

Steamed Sea Bream with Ginger

SERVES 2

2 sea bream, each weighing about
   400 g/14 oz, cleaned and scaled,
   heads removed
juice of 1 lime
1 tbsp fish sauce
2 tbsp groundnut oil, plus extra
   for brushing
4 spring onions, green parts included,
   shredded
3-cm/1¼-inch piece fresh ginger,
   sliced into very thin matchsticks

SPICE PASTE

1 tsp coriander seeds
½ tsp cumin seeds
1 tsp white peppercorns
¼ tsp salt
1-cm/½-inch piece fresh ginger, very
   finely chopped

TO GARNISH

small sprigs of fresh coriander
1 fresh red chilli, deseeded and
   thinly sliced
lime wedges

1. Using a sharp knife, make two diagonal slashes on each side of the fish. Put in a
   baking dish in a single layer. Sprinkle with the lime juice and fish sauce, rubbing the
   mixture over the skin and into the slashes. Leave to marinate for 15 minutes.

2. To make the spice paste, dry-fry the coriander seeds over a medium–high heat,
   shaking the pan frequently, for 2 minutes, or until starting to pop. Dry-fry the cumin
   seeds for 30 seconds or until fragrant, taking care not to let them burn. Combine
   with the remaining ingredients and grind to a paste using a mortar and pestle.
   Push the mixture into the slashes and rub the rest over the skin.

3. Brush two large pieces of thick foil with oil. Place a fish on each piece, along with
   any spice paste and liquid left in the dish. Sprinkle with the spring onion shreds.
   Make a loose parcel, sealing the edges well, and leave to stand for 15 minutes.
   Meanwhile, preheat the oven to 240°C/475°F/Gas Mark 9. Put a baking tray in the
   oven to heat. Place the fish on the preheated tray and bake for 10 minutes, then
   turn the parcels over and bake for a further 5 minutes.

4. Meanwhile, heat the oil in a small frying pan over a medium–high heat. Add the
   ginger matchsticks and fry for 1½ –2 minutes until golden. Drain on crumpled
   kitchen paper. Transfer the fish parcels to serving plates and open them up. Serve
   immediately, sprinkled with the ginger and garnished with coriander, chilli slices
   and lime wedges.

Spiced Tuna in Sweet-and-Sour Sauce

SERVES 4

4 fresh tuna steaks, about
   500 g/1 lb 2 oz in total

¼ tsp pepper

2 tbsp groundnut oil

1 onion, diced

1 small red pepper, deseeded and cut
   into short thin sticks

1 garlic clove, crushed

½ cucumber, deseeded and cut into
   short thin sticks

2 pineapple slices, diced

1 tsp finely chopped fresh ginger

1 tbsp soft light brown sugar

1 tbsp cornflour

1½ tbsp lime juice

1 tbsp Thai fish sauce

300 ml/10 fl oz fish stock

lime slices and cucumber slices,
   to garnish

1. Sprinkle the tuna steaks with pepper on both sides. Heat a heavy-based frying pan or ridged griddle pan and brush with a little oil. Arrange the tuna steaks in the pan and cook for 8 minutes, turning once.

2. Meanwhile, heat the remaining oil in a separate frying pan. Add the onion, pepper and garlic and cook gently for 3–4 minutes to soften.

3. Remove the pan from the heat and stir in the cucumber, pineapple, ginger and sugar.

4. Blend the cornflour with the lime juice and fish sauce, then stir into the stock and add to the pan. Stir over a medium heat until boiling, then cook for 1–2 minutes, or until thickened and clear.

5. Spoon the sauce over the tuna and serve immediately, garnished with slices of lime and cucumber.

Spicy Seafood Stew

SERVES 4

200 g/7 oz squid, cleaned and tentacles discarded

500 g/1 lb 2 oz firm white fish fillet, preferably monkfish or halibut

1 tbsp corn oil

4 shallots, finely chopped

2 garlic cloves, finely chopped

2 tbsp Green Curry Paste (see page 11)

2 small lemon grass stems, finely chopped

1 tsp shrimp paste

500 ml/16 fl oz coconut milk

200 g/7 oz raw king prawns, peeled and deveined

12 live clams in shells, cleaned

8 fresh basil leaves, finely shredded

fresh basil leaves, to garnish

freshly cooked rice, to serve

1. Using a sharp knife, cut the squid body cavities into thick rings and the white fish into bite-sized chunks.

2. Heat the oil in a large preheated wok. Add the shallots, garlic and curry paste and stir-fry for 1–2 minutes. Add the lemon grass and shrimp paste, then stir in the coconut milk and bring to the boil.

3. Reduce the heat until the liquid is simmering gently, then add the squid, white fish and prawns to the wok and simmer for 2 minutes.

4. Add the clams and simmer for a further minute or until the clams have opened. Discard any clams that remain closed.

5. Sprinkle the shredded basil leaves over the stew. Transfer to serving plates, then garnish with whole basil leaves and serve immediately with freshly cooked rice.

Marinated Fried Scallops

SERVES 4

20 scallops
1 tbsp groundnut oil
1 tbsp toasted sesame oil
squeeze of lime juice
1 tbsp chopped fresh coriander,
   to garnish
1 tbsp chopped fresh mint, to garnish
lime wedges, to serve

MARINADE
juice of 1 lime
1 fresh red chilli, deseeded and thinly
   sliced
2 tsp light soy sauce
2 tsp Thai fish sauce
1 tsp sugar
¼ tsp pepper

1. Put the scallops in a shallow dish. Combine the marinade ingredients and
   pour over the scallops, tossing to coat. Cover and leave in the refrigerator for
   30 minutes or up to 2 hours.

2. Heat a wok over a high heat and add the groundnut oil and sesame oil. Add the
   scallops and stir-fry with any juices from the marinade for 4–5 minutes until cooked
   through. Sprinkle with a squeeze of lime juice. Tip into a warmed serving dish
   along with any pan juices, then garnish with coriander and mint and serve with
   lime wedges.

Prawns with Coconut Rice

SERVES 4

115 g/4 oz dried Chinese mushrooms

2 tbsp vegetable oil or groundnut oil

6 spring onions, chopped

55 g/2 oz desiccated coconut

1 fresh green chilli, deseeded and chopped

225 g/8 oz jasmine rice

150 ml/5 fl oz fish stock

400 ml/14 fl oz coconut milk

350 g/12 oz cooked peeled prawns

6 sprigs fresh Thai basil

1. Place the mushrooms in a small bowl, cover with hot water and set aside to soak for 30 minutes. Drain, then cut off and discard the stalks and slice the caps.

2. Heat 1 tablespoon of the oil in a wok, add the spring onions, coconut and chilli and stir-fry for 2–3 minutes until lightly browned. Add the mushrooms and stir-fry for 3–4 minutes.

3. Add the rice and stir-fry for 2–3 minutes, then add the stock and bring to the boil. Reduce the heat and add the coconut milk. Simmer for 10–15 minutes, until the rice is tender. Stir in the prawns and basil, heat through and serve.

Prawn Noodle Bowl

SERVES 4

1 bunch spring onions

2 celery sticks

1 red pepper

200 g/7 oz vermicelli rice noodles

2 tbsp groundnut oil

55 g/2 oz unsalted peanuts

1 fresh bird's eye chilli, sliced

1 lemon grass stem, crushed

400 ml/14 fl oz fish stock or chicken stock

200 ml/7 fl oz coconut milk

2 tsp Thai fish sauce

350 g/12 oz cooked peeled tiger prawns

salt and pepper

3 tbsp chopped fresh coriander, to garnish

1. Trim the spring onions and celery and thinly slice diagonally. Deseed and thinly slice the red pepper.

2. Place the noodles in a bowl, cover with boiling water and leave to stand for 4 minutes, or until tender. Drain. Heat the oil in a wok, add the peanuts and stir-fry for 1–2 minutes until golden. Lift out with a slotted spoon. Add the sliced vegetables to the wok and stir-fry over a high heat for 1–2 minutes. Add the chilli, lemon grass, stock, coconut milk and fish sauce and bring to the boil.

3. Stir in the prawns and bring back to the boil, stirring. Season to taste with salt and pepper, then add the noodles. Serve in warmed bowls, sprinkled with fresh coriander.

Egg-fried Rice With Prawns and Peppers

SERVES 4

225 g/8 oz jasmine rice

1 tbsp groundnut oil or vegetable oil

2 spring onions, finely chopped

2 eggs, beaten

handful of fresh coriander, chopped,
plus extra sprigs to garnish

PRAWNS AND PEPPERS

55 g/2 oz creamed coconut

150 ml/5 fl oz boiling water

4 tbsp groundnut oil or vegetable oil

2 fresh red chillies, deseeded and
roughly chopped

6 spring onions, roughly chopped

350 g/12 oz cooked peeled prawns

juice of ½ lemon

6 fresh Thai basil leaves, torn

1 tbsp Thai fish sauce

1 red pepper, deseeded and
cut into strips

1. Bring a large saucepan of lightly salted water to the boil, add the rice and cook for 12–15 minutes, or until just tender. Rinse under cold running water, fluff up with a fork and leave to cool completely.

2. Heat the oil in a preheated wok, add the spring onions and stir-fry over a medium–high heat for 30 seconds. Add the rice and stir-fry for 1–2 minutes, or until heated through. Push all the rice to one side of the wok and tilt the pan to allow any oil to run to the opposite side. While still tilted, add the eggs and cook over a medium heat, stirring constantly, for 2–3 minutes until set. Return the wok to a level position, add the coriander and stir the rice through the cooked eggs. Remove from the heat but keep the rice warm in the wok.

3. For the prawns and peppers, chop the creamed coconut and dissolve in the boiling water. Heat half the oil in a separate preheated wok, add the chillies and spring onions and stir-fry over a medium–high heat for 1–2 minutes until just tender. Add the prawns, coconut mixture, lemon juice, basil and fish sauce and bring gently to the boil, stirring occasionally, to ensure that the prawns are heated through.

4. Heat the remaining oil in a small frying pan, add the red pepper and stir-fry over a high heat for 1–2 minutes until sizzling and lightly browned. Stir into the prawn mixture and serve immediately with the egg-fried rice, garnished with coriander.

Chilli Prawns with Garlic Noodles

SERVES 4

200 g/7 oz cooked, peeled and
   deveined king or tiger prawns

4 tbsp sweet chilli dipping sauce

4 tbsp groundnut oil or vegetable oil

4 spring onions, chopped

55 g/2 oz mangetout, trimmed and
   halved diagonally

1 tbsp Red Curry Paste (see page 11)

400 ml/14 fl oz coconut milk

55 g/2 oz canned, drained
   bamboo shoots

55 g/2 oz fresh beansprouts

GARLIC NOODLES

115 g/4 oz dried medium egg noodles

2 garlic cloves, crushed

handful of fresh coriander, chopped

1. Toss the prawns with the chilli sauce in a bowl. Cover and set aside.

2. Heat half the oil in a preheated wok, add the spring onions and mangetout and stir-fry over a medium–high heat for 2–3 minutes. Add the curry paste and stir well. Pour in the coconut milk and bring gently to the boil, stirring occasionally. Add the bamboo shoots and beansprouts and cook, stirring, for 1 minute. Stir in the prawns and chilli sauce, reduce the heat and simmer for 1–2 minutes until just heated through.

3. Meanwhile, for the garlic noodles, bring a large a saucepan of lightly salted water to the boil, add the noodles and cook for 4–5 minutes, or until just tender. Drain and return to the saucepan.

4. Heat the remaining oil in a small, non-stick frying pan, add the garlic and stir-fry over a high heat for 30 seconds. Add to the drained noodles with half the coriander and toss together until well mixed.

5. Transfer the garlic noodles to four serving bowls, top with the chilli prawn mixture and serve immediately, garnished with the remaining coriander.

Prawn and Pineapple Curry

SERVES 4

½ fresh pineapple

400 ml/14 fl oz coconut cream

2 tbsp Red Curry Paste (see page 11)

2 tbsp Thai fish sauce

2 tsp sugar

350 g/12 oz raw tiger prawns

2 tbsp chopped coriander

steamed jasmine rice, to serve

1. Peel the pineapple and chop the flesh. Heat the coconut cream, pineapple, curry paste, fish sauce and sugar in a wok or saucepan until almost boiling.

2. Shell and devein the prawns. Add the prawns and chopped coriander to the wok and simmer for 3 minutes, or until the prawns are cooked – they will turn a bright pink colour.

3. Serve the prawns with steamed jasmine rice

Stir-fried Squid with Hot Black Bean Sauce

SERVES 4

750 g/1 lb 10 oz squid, cleaned and
   tentacles discarded

1 large red pepper, deseeded

115 g/4 oz mangetout

1 head pak choi

1½ tbsp corn oil

1 small fresh red bird's-eye chilli,
   chopped

1 garlic clove, finely chopped

1 tsp grated fresh ginger

2 spring onions, chopped

BLACK BEAN SAUCE

3 tbsp black bean sauce

1 tbsp Thai fish sauce

1 tbsp rice wine or dry sherry

1 tbsp dark soy sauce

1 tsp soft light brown sugar

1 tsp cornflour

1 tbsp water

1. Cut the squid body cavities into quarters lengthways. Use the tip of a small, sharp knife to score a diamond pattern into the flesh without cutting all the way through. Pat dry with kitchen paper

2. Cut the red pepper into long, thin slices. Cut the mangetout in half diagonally. Coarsely shred the pak choi.

3. To make the sauce, mix the black bean sauce, fish sauce, rice wine, soy sauce and sugar together in a bowl. Blend the cornflour with the water and stir into the other ingredients in the bowl. Reserve the mixture until required.

4. Heat the oil in a preheated wok. Add the chilli, garlic, ginger and spring onions and stir-fry for 1 minute. Add the red pepper and stir-fry for 2 minutes.

5. Add the squid and stir-fry over a high heat for a further minute. Stir in the mangetout and pak choi and stir for a further minute, or until wilted.

6. Stir in the sauce ingredients and cook, stirring constantly, for 2 minutes or until the sauce thickens and clears. Serve immediately.

Index

asparagus: red curry with mixed
  leaves 62
aubergines 10
  duck jungle curry 146
  green chicken curry 125
  green fish curry 161
  red chicken curry 126

bamboo shoots
  chilli prawns with garlic
    noodles 185
  duck jungle curry 146
  ginger chicken with noodles 134
  pork and prawn spring rolls 37
  seven-spice chicken with
    courgettes 138
  tom yum soup with fish 29
beansprouts
  caramelized tuna salad 82
  chicken-coconut soup 22
  chilli prawns with garlic noodles 185
  fish curry with rice noodles 162
  mixed fish and coconut curry 165
  pad thai 100
  peppered beef salad 73
  pork and prawn spring rolls 37
  spring vegetable rice 65
  stir-fry with duck and peas 150
  vegetable and black bean spring
    rolls 46
beef
  beef with black pepper and lime 96
  beef and noodle soup 17
  coconut beef curry 92
  hot beef and coconut curry 99
  marinated beef with celery 95
  masaman curry 91
  peppered beef salad 73
  spicy beef and mushroom wontons 33
black bean sauce 46, 189
broccoli
  broccoli with peanuts 54
  hot and sour vegetable salad 85
  vegetable stir-fry 61

cabbage
  cabbage and coconut curry 70
  red chicken salad 77
carrots
  carrot and pumpkin curry 66
  crab cakes 41
  duck with spring onion soup 25
  ginger chicken with noodles 134
  hot and sour vegetable salad 85
  mixed fish and coconut curry 165
  spicy prawn soup 26
  spring vegetable rice 65
  vegetable and black bean spring rolls 46
  vegetable stir-fry 61
cashew nuts
  cauliflower and beans with cashew
    nuts 57
  pork stir-fry with cashew nuts, lime
    and mint 107
cauliflower: cauliflower and beans with
  cashew nuts 57
celery
  marinated beef with celery 95
  prawn noodle bowl 181
  tofu and vegetable curry 69
chicken
  chicken curry with fried noodles 137
  chicken noodle soup 21

chicken and peanut curry 141
chicken satay skewers 38
chicken with vegetables and
  coriander rice 133
chicken-coconut soup 22
ginger chicken with noodles 134
gingered chicken and vegetable
  salad 74
green chicken curry 125
red chicken curry 126
red chicken salad 77
seven-spice chicken with courgettes 138
shredded chicken and mixed
  mushrooms 142
Thai chicken 130
yellow chicken curry 129
chillies 10
  beef with black pepper and lime 96
  broccoli with peanuts 54
  cabbage and coconut curry 70
  carrot and pumpkin curry 66
  chicken curry with fried noodles 137
  chicken noodle soup 21
  chicken-coconut soup 22
  crab cakes 41
  crisp-fried spicy turkey 145
  crispy pork dumplings 34
  crispy roast duck and pickled plums
    154
  duck with chilli jam and deep-fried
    shallots 149
  egg-fried rice with prawns and
    peppers 182
  green curry paste 11
  hot and sour soup 30
  hot beef and coconut curry 99
  lamb with lime leaves 116
  marinated beef with celery 95
  marinated fried scallops 177
  mushroom and tofu laksa with
    noodles 58
  pad thai 100
  peppered beef salad 73
  pork and vegetable broth 18
  prawn noodle bowl 181
  prawns with coconut rice 178
  red chicken curry 126
  red curry paste 11
  seven-spice chicken with courgettes 138
  spicy prawn soup 26
  stir-fried lamb with mint 119
  stir-fried squid with hot black bean
    sauce 189
  stir-fry with duck and peas 150
  swordfish kebabs 169
  tofu and vegetable curry 69
  tom yum soup with fish 29
Chinese leaves
  beef with black pepper and lime 96
  red chicken salad 77
  red curry with mixed leaves 62
coconut cream/milk
  cabbage and coconut curry 70
  carrot and pumpkin curry 66
  chicken curry with fried noodles 137
  chicken and peanut curry 141
  chicken with vegetables and
    coriander rice 133
  chicken-coconut soup 22
  chilli prawns with garlic noodles 185
  coconut beef curry 92
  egg-fried rice with prawns and
    peppers 182

fish curry with rice noodles 162
green chicken curry 125
green fish curry 161
hot beef and coconut curry 99
lamb with lime leaves 116
masaman curry 91
mixed fish and coconut curry 165
mushroom and tofu laksa with
  noodles 58
prawn noodle bowl 181
prawn and pineapple curry 186
prawns with coconut rice 178
red chicken curry 126
red curry with mixed leaves 62
red lamb curry 115
red pork curry with peppers 104
sea bass and mango salad 81
spicy seafood stew 174
tofu and vegetable curry 69
cooking equipment 9
coriander
  cabbage and coconut curry 70
  caramelized tuna salad 82
  chicken curry with fried noodles 1
  chilli prawns with garlic noodles 1
  crab cakes 41
  duck with chilli jam and deep-fried
    shallots 149
  egg-fried rice with prawns and
    peppers 182
  green curry paste 11
  hot beef and coconut curry 99
  lamb with lime leaves 116
  masaman curry 91
  minced pork kebabs with sweet c
    dipping sauce 111
  mixed fish and coconut curry 165
  monkfish kebabs with red peppe
    and prawns 166
  mushroom and tofu laksa with noodl
  pad thai 100
  prawn and pineapple curry 186
  red curry with mixed leaves 62
  red curry paste 11
  red lamb curry 115
  red roasted pork with peppered
    noodles 108
  sea bass and mango salad 81
  seven-spice chicken with courget
    138
  spicy parcels 45
  spicy prawn soup 26
  spring vegetable rice 65
  swordfish kebabs 169
  tom yum soup with fish 29
  yellow chicken curry 129
coriander root 10
courgettes
  crab cakes 41
  duck jungle curry 146
  seven-spice chicken with courget
    138
crab cakes 41
cucumber
  caramelized tuna salad 82
  chicken and peanut curry 141
  duck salad 78
  gingered chicken and vegetable sala
  mixed vegetables with basil 53
  spiced tuna in sweet and sour
    sauce 173
  vegetable and black bean spring
    rolls 46

pastes *see individual types*

o-frying technique 8

spy roast duck and pickled plums
  54
ck with chilli jam and deep-fried
  hallots 149
ck jungle curry 146
ck with mixed peppers 153
ck salad 78
ck with spring onion soup 25
-fry with duck and peas 150

g-fried rice with prawns and
  peppers 182
d thai 100
icy parcels 45

sauce 10
and seafood
  ab cakes 41
h curry with rice noodles 162
een fish curry 161
arinated fried scallops 177
xed fish and coconut curry 165
icy parcels 45
icy seafood stew 174
eamed sea bream with ginger 170
ordfish kebabs 169
m yum soup with fish 29
e *also* monkfish; prawns; squid; tuna
ch beans
occoli with peanuts 54
xed fish and coconut curry 165

ngal 10
rrot and pumpkin curry 66
ck with chilli jam and deep-fried
  hallots 149
ck jungle curry 146
een lamb stir-fry with noodles and
  peanuts 112
m yum soup with fish 29
ger
eef and noodle soup 17
occoli with peanuts 54
bbage and coconut curry 70
icken noodle soup 21
icken satay skewers 38
icken with vegetables and
  coriander rice 133
icken-coconut soup 22
ck with chilli jam and deep-fried
  shallots 149
ck jungle curry 146
ck with spring onion soup 25
nger chicken with noodles 134
ngered chicken and vegetable salad 74
een lamb stir-fry with noodles and
  peanuts 112
t and sour vegetable salad 85
ushroom and tofu laksa with
  noodles 58
eppered beef salad 73
ork stir-fry with cashew nuts, lime
  and mint 107
ork and vegetable broth 18
d curry paste 11
d roasted pork with peppered
  noodles 108
ven-spice chicken with courgettes
  138
redded chicken and mixed
  mushrooms 142

spiced tuna in sweet and sour sauce 173
spicy prawn soup 26
steamed sea bream with ginger 170
stir-fried squid with hot black bean
  sauce 189
stir-fry with duck and peas 150
swordfish kebabs 169
tom yum soup with fish 29
vegetable and black bean spring
  rolls 46
vegetable stir-fry 61
green curry paste 11
  broccoli with peanuts 54
  chicken curry with fried noodles 137
  duck jungle curry 146
  green chicken curry 125
  green fish curry 161
  green lamb stir-fry with noodles and
    peanuts 112
  shredded chicken and mixed
    mushrooms 142
  spicy parcels 45
  spicy seafood stew 174

hot and sour soup 30
hot and sour vegetable salad 85

ingredients 9–10

kaffir lime leaves 10
  broccoli with peanuts 54
  chicken curry with fried noodles 137
  chicken noodle soup 21
  chicken and peanut curry 141
  chicken-coconut soup 22
  coconut beef curry 92
  green chicken curry 125
  green curry paste 11
  green fish curry 161
  hot beef and coconut curry 99
  lamb with lime leaves 116
  red curry with mixed leaves 62
  red curry paste 11
  tom yum soup with fish 29

lamb
  green lamb stir-fry with noodles and
    peanuts 112
  lamb with lime leaves 116
  red lamb curry 115
  stir-fried lamb with mint 119
leeks: chicken noodle soup 21
lemon grass 10
  broccoli with peanuts 54
  carrot and pumpkin curry 66
  chicken noodle soup 21
  chicken and peanut curry 141
  chicken-coconut soup 22
  duck salad 78
  green chicken curry 125
  green curry paste 11
  hot and sour soup 30
  lamb with lime leaves 116
  mushroom and tofu laksa with
    noodles 58
  peppered beef salad 73
  pork and vegetable broth 18
  prawn noodle bowl 181
  red chicken curry 126
  red curry paste 11
  spicy prawn soup 26
  spicy seafood stew 174
  swordfish kebabs 169
  tom yum soup with fish 29
  vegetable stir-fry 61
limes

beef with black pepper and lime 96
beef and noodle soup 17
cabbage and coconut curry 70
chicken-coconut soup 22
duck jungle curry 146
hot and sour soup 30
marinated fried scallops 177
monkfish kebabs with red peppers
  and prawns 166
pad thai 100
pork stir-fry with cashew nuts, lime
  and mint 107
red curry paste 11
red lamb curry 115
spiced tuna in sweet and sour sauce
  173
steamed sea bream with ginger 170
stir-fry with duck and peas 150
swordfish kebabs 169
tom yum soup with fish 29

macadamia nuts 58
Madras curry paste: stir-fried lamb with
  mint 119
mangetout
  chicken with vegetables and
    coriander rice 133
  chilli prawns with garlic noodles 185
  gingered chicken and vegetable
    salad 74
  hot and sour vegetable salad 85
  mixed vegetables with basil 53
  spring vegetable rice 65
  stir-fried squid with hot black bean
    sauce 189
  stir-fry with duck and peas 150
mangoes: sea bass and mango salad 81
masaman curry paste
  coconut beef curry 92
  masaman curry 91
menu planning 8
monkfish
  fish curry with rice noodles 162
  monkfish kebabs with red peppers
    and prawns 166
mushrooms
  chicken curry with fried noodles 137
  chicken with vegetables and
    coriander rice 133
  duck with spring onion soup 25
  fish curry with rice noodles 162
  hot and sour soup 30
  mixed vegetables with basil 53
  mushroom and tofu laksa with
    noodles 58
  pork and prawn spring rolls 37
  prawns with coconut rice 178
  red pork curry with peppers 104
  shredded chicken and mixed
    mushrooms 142
  spicy beef and mushroom wontons 33
  spicy prawn soup 26
  tofu and vegetable curry 69

nam pla 10
noodles
  beef and noodle soup 17
  chicken curry with fried noodles 137
  chicken noodle soup 21
  chicken-coconut soup 22
  chilli prawns with garlic noodles 185
  fish curry with rice noodles 162
  ginger chicken with noodles 134
  gingered chicken and vegetable salad 74
  green lamb stir-fry with noodles and
    peanuts 112

mixed fish and coconut curry 165
mushroom and tofu laksa with noodles 58
pad thai 100
pork and vegetable broth 18
prawn noodle bowl 181
red roasted pork with peppered
noodles 108
spicy prawn soup 26
vegetable stir-fry 61

oyster sauce 103, 154

pad thai 100
pak choi
chicken with vegetables and
coriander rice 133
hot and sour soup 30
red chicken salad 77
red curry with mixed leaves 62
spicy parcels 45
stir-fried squid with hot black bean
sauce 189
palm sugar 10
peanuts
broccoli with peanuts 54
caramelized tuna salad 82
chicken and peanut curry 141
chicken satay skewers 38
coconut beef curry 92
crisp-fried spicy turkey 145
green lamb stir-fry with noodles and
peanuts 112
masaman curry 91
pad thai 100
prawn noodle bowl 181
red chicken curry 126
peas: stir-fry with duck and peas 150
Penang curry paste: chicken and
peanut curry 141
peppers
broccoli with peanuts 54
duck with mixed peppers 153
duck with spring onion soup 25
egg-fried rice with prawns and
peppers 182
gingered chicken and vegetable
salad 74
hot and sour vegetable salad 85
marinated beef with celery 95
mixed vegetable with basil 53
monkfish kebabs with red peppers
and prawns 166
peppered beef salad 73
pork stir-fry with cashew nuts, lime
and mint 107
pork and vegetable broth 18
prawn noodle bowl 181
red chicken curry 126
red lamb curry 115
red pork curry with peppers 104
red roasted pork with peppered
noodles 108
seven-spice chicken with courgettes
138
spiced tuna in sweet and sour sauce 173
stir-fried squid with hot black bean
sauce 189
swordfish kebabs 169
tofu and vegetable curry 69
vegetable and black bean spring
rolls 46
pineapple
chicken and peanut curry 141
duck salad 78
prawn and pineapple curry 186
spiced tuna in sweet and sour sauce 173

plums: crispy roast duck and pickled
plums 154
pork
caramelized belly pork with star
anise 103
crispy pork dumplings 34
minced pork kebabs with sweet chilli
dipping sauce 111
pad thai 100
pork and prawn spring rolls 37
pork stir-fry with cashew nuts, lime
and mint 107
pork and vegetable broth 18
red pork curry with peppers 104
red roasted pork with peppered
noodles 108
potatoes: masaman curry 91
prawns
chilli prawns with garlic noodles 185
crispy sesame prawns 42
egg-fried rice with prawns and
peppers 182
mixed fish and coconut curry 165
monkfish kebabs with red peppers
and prawns 166
pad thai 100
pork and prawn spring rolls 37
prawn noodle bowl 181
prawn and pineapple curry 186
prawns with coconut rice 178
spicy parcels 45
spicy prawn soup 26
spicy seafood stew 174
tom yum soup with fish 29
pumpkin: carrot and pumpkin curry 66

red curry paste 11
cauliflower and beans with cashew
nuts 57
chilli prawns with garlic
noodles 185
crispy sesame prawns 42
duck salad 78
duck with spring onion soup 25
fish curry with rice noodles 162
hot beef and coconut curry 99
mixed fish and coconut curry 165
monkfish kebabs with red peppers
and prawns 166
prawn and pineapple curry 186
red chicken curry 126
red chicken salad 77
red curry with mixed leaves 62
red lamb curry 115
red pork curry with peppers 104
red roasted pork with peppered
noodles 108
sea bass and mango salad 81
spring vegetable rice 65
tofu and vegetable curry 69
vegetable stir-fry 61
regional cuisines 7
rice
chicken with vegetables and
coriander rice 133
egg-fried rice with prawns and
peppers 182
prawns with coconut rice 178
spring vegetable rice 65
runner beans: cauliflower and beans
with cashew nuts 57

sea bass and mango salad 81
sesame seeds
crab cakes 41
crispy sesame prawns 42

spring vegetable rice 65
seven-spice chicken with courgettes
shrimp paste 10
spices, grinding 8
spinach
red curry with mixed leaves 62
tofu and vegetable curry 69
spring rolls
pork and prawn spring rolls 37
vegetable and black bean spring
rolls 46
squid
mixed fish and coconut curry 165
spicy parcels 45
spicy seafood stew 174
stir-fried squid with hot black bea
sauce 189
stir-frying technique 8
sweetcorn
gingered chicken and vegetable
salad 74
hot and sour vegetable salad 85
mixed vegetables with basil 53
spring vegetable rice 65
stir-fried lamb with mint 119
tofu and vegetable curry 69
vegetable stir-fry 61
yellow chicken curry 129

tamarind paste 82, 116
Thai basil
crisp-fried spicy turkey 145
duck jungle curry 146
egg-fried rice with prawns and
peppers 182
gingered chicken and vegetable
salad 74
green fish curry 161
hot beef and coconut curry 99
mixed vegetables with basil 53
red lamb curry 115
sea bass and mango salad 81
spicy seafood stew 174
tips and techniques 8
tofu
hot and sour soup 30
mushroom and tofu laksa with noodle
tofu and vegetable curry 69
tomatoes
duck with mixed peppers 153
duck salad 78
lamb with lime leaves 116
red pork curry with peppers 104
tom yum soup with fish 29
tuna
caramelized tuna salad 82
spiced tuna in sweet and sour sauce
turkey: crisp-fried spicy turkey 145

water chestnuts
mixed vegetables with basil 53
pork and vegetable broth 18
red lamb curry 115
tom yum soup with fish 29
vegetable and black bean spring rol
vegetable stir-fry 61
wontons
crispy pork dumplings 34
spicy beef and mushroom wontons

yellow curry paste
carrot and pumpkin curry 66
yellow chicken curry 129